GW00367198

ROUZEGAR E NOW LTD.
NEW SOUTH WALES HOUSE
15 ADAM STREET, THE STRAND
LONDON WC2N 6AH

Saudis in Transition

The Challenges of a Changing Labor Market

A JOINT STUDY BY
THE MINISTRY OF PLANNING OF SAUDI ARABIA
AND THE WORLD BANK

SAUDI ARABIA
THE FIVE PLANNING REGIONS

Planning region boundaries
⊙ National centers
○ Regional centers
▨ Occupied territories

JORDAN
40°
IRAQ
ISRAEL
Sakaka
Neutral Zone
KUWAIT
30°
NORTHERN REGION
Tabuk
EASTERN
Hail
Persian
REGION
Jubail
BAHRAIN
Burayda
Dammam
CENTRAL
Al Khobar
QATAR
WESTERN
Medina
Riyadh
Hofuf
Yanbu
REGION
REGION
Mubaraz
ARAB REP. OF EGYPT
UNITED ARAB EMIRATES
Jeddah
Mecca
Taif
Al Baha
Bisha
20°
SUDAN
Red Sea
SOUTHWESTERN
OMAN
Qunfuda
REGION
Muhayl
Abha
Khamis Mushayt
Dhahran Al Janoub
Najran
Jizan
PEOPLE'S DEMOCRATIC REPUBLIC OF YEMEN
YEMEN ARAB
Arabian Sea
REPUBLIC
ETHIOPIA
0   200   400
40°
Gulf of Aden
50°
KILOMETERS

Saudis in Transition

The Challenges of a Changing Labor Market

Ismail A. Sirageldin

Naiem A. Sherbiny

M. Ismail Serageldin

Published for The World Bank
Oxford University Press

Oxford University Press

NEW YORK OXFORD LONDON GLASGOW
TORONTO MELBOURNE WELLINGTON HONG KONG
TOKYO KUALA LUMPUR SINGAPORE JAKARTA
DELHI BOMBAY CALCUTTA MADRAS KARACHI
NAIROBI DAR ES SALAAM CAPE TOWN

First printing September 1984

EDITOR   Jane H. Carroll
FIGURES   Catherine Kocak
COVER DESIGN   Joyce C. Eisen

Library of Congress Cataloging in Publication Data

Sirageldin, Ismail Abdel-Hamid.
  Saudis in transition.

  Includes index.
  1. Labor supply—Saudi Arabia. I. Sherbiny,
Naiem A. II. Serageldin, Ismail, 1944–
III. World Bank. IV. Title.
HD5812.35.A6S57   1984   331.12'0953'8   84-1104
ISBN 0-19-520457-3

Contents

Preface

THIS BOOK IS BASED on a study undertaken jointly by the Ministry of Planning of Saudi Arabia and the World Bank. The study was initiated at the suggestion of Dr. Faisal Al-Bashir, then deputy minister of planning. His advice and guidance throughout the various phases of the original work and his review and clearance of the manuscript underlying the present volume are deeply appreciated.

The study was an attempt to understand the main variables and processes in the shifting conditions of the labor market of Saudi Arabia during the late 1970s. In exploring such factors as labor's mobility between locations and jobs, wage determination, job search, and skill formation, the study generated a broad base of information on various institutional aspects of the Saudi labor market. To make these important new findings more widely available, a scholarly publication was suggested that would highlight features of a rapidly changing labor market caught in transition from tradition to modernity. By necessity, the present book reports on a small fraction of the findings of the study. The material herein is organized around the theme of the response of Saudi nationals to the rapidly changing conditions of a domestic labor market which is becoming increasingly international. Although the findings were based on a single snapshot taken during the survey of 1978, the questions posed to the respondents included both retrospective and prospective dimensions that enabled the authors to establish some trends and capture the essence of a dynamic process.

The first draft of this manuscript was reviewed by Dr. Al-Bashir and a number of his colleagues and advisers in the Ministry of Planning. Their comments have all been gratefully accepted and incorporated in the present version.

As we bring this effort before the wider public, we wish to record our thanks to and appreciation of the many colleagues without whom this work could not have been completed. In Saudi Arabia, although thanks are due to many, we would like to mention specifically Dr. Faisal Al-Bashir; Hussein Sageni, at present deputy minister of planning in Saudi Arabia, who was assistant deputy minister of planning at the time of the study; and Dr. Hussein Mansour, chairman of the Saudi Commission for Manpower Planning, formerly assistant deputy minister for national planning at the time of the study. At the World Bank, the authors are most indebted to the originality and untiring support of staff members Michael Wilson, James Socknat, Murti Pemmarazu, and Narong Thananart and consultants David King and James Scoville. The field survey, the source of all the data, could not have been carried out without George Vassiliou and his Middle East Marketing Research Bureau, who ably executed the demanding field work and organized the complex analysis of the data. With special appreciation, we have incorporated the valuable comments received from the reviewers appointed by the Bank's Editorial Subcommittee. Finally, we gratefully acknowledge the outstanding editorial assistance of Richard R. Herbert.

Saudis in Transition

The Challenges of a Changing Labor Market

1. Introduction

SAUDI ARABIA in recent years has become the very embodiment of a society in transition, caught somewhere between tradition and modernity. Nowhere is this dilemma better manifested than in the country's rapidly changing labor market. Until the late 1930s, when oil was discovered in commercial quantities, Saudi Arabia was a typically traditional society.[1] Little or no change had taken place for hundreds of years. Its distinguished international role was as the domicile of the Ka'aba, the most sacred shrine of Islam. Hundreds of thousands of pilgrims to Mecca performed the rituals every year, as they had for fourteen centuries, providing an important source of revenue, but having little or no impact on the development of the country's economic base.

The Context

The process of modernization began to pick up speed in the late 1950s, but only in the early 1970s did matters change dramatically as Saudi Arabia was thrust into the international limelight with a new and strategic role as the largest exporter of crude oil and the de facto leader of the Organization of Petroleum Exporting Countries (OPEC). The substantial gain in the strategic importance of OPEC after the Middle East war of 1973 gave Saudi Arabia a special stature in the world of politics and diplomacy. The quadrupling of oil prices produced substantial capital flows into the coffers of the oil exporters, who were not able to absorb all the capital domestically. The resulting phenomenon of the capital-surplus oil-exporting countries was nowhere better manifested than in Saudi Arabia, which earned a special status in the world of commerce and finance by its accumulation of large surpluses. Saudi policymakers seized the opportunity of capital availability in unprecedented quantities and, during the 1970s, launched some of the most ambitious development plans the developing world has ever known. Witness are the overall and sectoral growth targets of the first five-year plan (1970–75) which were formulated in the late 1960s under capital-scarcity constraint.[2] By the end of the first

3

plan in 1975, all the previously set growth targets were exceeded by the actual performance of the economy.[3] The second development plan (1975–80)[4] set even more ambitious growth targets, and the record shows that most targets were achieved and some were surpassed.[5]

This deliberate acceleration of growth and structural change in the Saudi economy threw the domestic labor market into a turmoil. At the highest policymaking levels, a conscious decision was made to allow the inflow of as much expatriate labor as was necessary to achieve the adopted growth targets. Aware of the tradeoffs between minimizing the presence of expatriate labor and maximizing economic growth, policymakers appear to have opted for the latter during the 1970s. The underlying assumption was that while expatriates are more or less transitory, the benefits of economic growth can be made to last. Even though the government took the most active role in shaping conditions conducive for growth and structural change, the entire orientation of the economy, and the prevailing social philosophy, remained strongly committed to private enterprise. This orientation was naturally reflected in the labor market and its dynamics. Almost literally overnight, expatriate workers flocked to the Saudi labor market from neighboring countries and beyond.[6] The size, composition, and locus of the demand for labor have shifted dramatically. Unlike the situation in many other countries, especially those of Western Europe, expatriate labor was imported to Saudi Arabia, not to continue the pace of economic progress, but to accomplish the unprecedented task of reshaping the entire economy in the shortest possible time. Nowhere outside the capital-surplus oil countries had massive immigration been so impressively utilized to carry out what is possibly the largest-scale transformation of a developing economy in social history. It is for this reason that the Saudi labor market has undergone fundamental changes in such a short period.

Changes occurred simultaneously in the size, skill structure, location, and even practices of labor supply and demand. The traditionally closed and small Saudi labor market suddenly became wide open to significant labor inflows from numerous countries. By 1981, more than 2 million expatriates (about 30 percent of the total population) had poured in from around the world. No language or social barriers could stand in the way of these labor flows. With the rapid build-up of the socioeconomic infrastructure and diversification of the economy, expatriate workers covered nearly the entire spectrum of skills. Whether it was Yemeni construction laborers, Indian telex operators, Syrian teachers, Korean technicians, Egyptian doctors, or American engineers, they all found in the Saudi labor market an irresistible magnet representing ample and exciting opportunities. Unlike the concentration of expatriate labor in the big cities in Europe, expatriates in Saudi Arabia were found in both large cities and small towns alike. In fact, it became rather common for expatriates to be located literally in the middle of nowhere, to help start up new major economic activities and carve out new communities, such as the industrial centers of Jubail, amid the oil fields of the Gulf coast, and Yanbu, on the Red Sea coast.

This massive inflow of immigrants helped propel the country's immediate growth ambitions; it also created the potential for longer-term social, economic, and political tensions. Alien habits upset the locals, especially the Bedouin and peasant-farmer populations trying to tally traditional work and consumption patterns with the glossy fallout from the mass-consumption industrial West suddenly constructed all around them—skyscrapers, motorways, international banks and hotels, and an unlimited menu of the latest in consumer goods and durables. Indeed, the material standard of living of Saudis improved considerably during the second half of the 1970s; for example, average real earnings rose 71 percent during this period.[7] But accelerated development unavoidably generates differences in life chances and adversely affects economic equality.[8] Accordingly, welfare services, housing and social subsidies, and other types of transfer payments to Saudi workers and families became a significant part of public expenditure. These benefits were not equally available for expatriate workers. Disparities in working conditions, wages and salaries, and benefits between expatriate and Saudi workers and among the various nationalities created a new labor market segmented along nationality lines. New institutions dealing with labor placement and disputes were introduced. Even the legal framework[9] and social practices governing the behavior of workers in the market and organizing their individual relationships with employers underwent significant changes, as will be shown throughout this book.

As the economy modernized, the labor market evolved dynamically to suit the widely variant backgrounds of expatriate workers. It was not and is not a Saudi policy objective to rely indefinitely on expatriate workers, however. An important purpose of the development plans is to utilize as effectively as possible the existing local labor force and to develop a well-trained labor force of locals—and keep them at home. This is a long-term process that may take at least until the end of the century, if not beyond. The important question is: What effect(s) do these labor market dynamics have on the development of local human resources in the kingdom? More specific questions that are becoming increasingly important and comprise the core of this book are: How have Saudis been adjusting to the sudden and substantial increase in the demand for their labor? What is their response to investing in their own human capital through additional training and education? How do they respond to new opportunities that require geographic and occupational mobility? Is the resulting distribution of wages related to that of skills and training?

In fact, does the behavior of Saudis in the labor market conform to the maximizing behavior found in competitive markets? As will be discussed in chapter 2, which reviews conceptual issues in labor market analysis, there is no a priori reason to expect such competitive behavior. But in the final analysis the question is an empirical one. Hence an empirical investigation of the labor market in Saudi Arabia was undertaken by the Saudi Ministry of Planning and the World Bank. This book is derived from that study. Because of the complexity of the relationships, the empirical analysis is based mainly on multivariate techniques. It must be mentioned at the outset, however, that the models used in this book and their results should be viewed as exploratory and tentative. They are complemented by the informed judgments of the authors.

Background and Genesis of the Study

Human resource development has been a primary concern of the Saudi government through its recent history of socioeconomic planning. An integrated program for human resource development, including the institutional changes necessary to achieve the program targets, was outlined and discussed in the second plan.[10] The importance of those tasks called for immediate attempts to develop analytical tools to study, guide, and monitor human resource development in the kingdom, especially in the near future.

Within the framework of the Technical Cooperation Agreement between the Kingdom of Saudi Arabia and the World Bank, a major multistage study of the development of human resources in the kingdom was undertaken in the mid-1970s for the Ministry of Planning (MOP) by the World Bank. The main purpose of the inquiry was to develop an adequate understanding of, and initiate planning for, human resource development in the kingdom. One of several interrelated studies undertaken was the Compound Manpower Planning Model, which was designed to forecast and monitor Saudi and foreign labor requirements within a consistent framework of the Education and Training Systems (ETS), investment plans, and the importation of foreign labor.[11] Other, unpublished studies included the Critical Skills Survey of 1976 and a demographic forecasting exercise. There was, however, no information about the regional distribution of labor and the extent of interregional labor mobility, the degree of skill formation, or occupational mobility.

There was a serious information gap regarding the structure and operation of the labor market. Forecasts obtained from Manpower Planning
Models were conditional on parameters estimated without adequate
empirical foundation.

Several of the MOP-Bank joint studies focused mainly on the demand
side and to some extent on the demographic characteristics of the supply
side in Saudi Arabia. The studies examined the structure of capital
utilization, its requirements for various skills or human resources, and the
effect of a labor shortage on capacity utilization as implied in the distribution of vacancies by various levels of skill at a given point in time. Those
studies assembled valuable information about job vacancies, their duration, and management efforts in recruitment, especially for the skills
considered critical to the growth of the key industrial and social sectors.

Most of the above-mentioned studies provided important factual and
descriptive information on the Saudi labor market that had immediate
policy relevance to manpower planning. For example, the Critical Skills
Survey concluded that manpower shortages were pervasive in the public
and private sectors and threatened to thwart the effective implementation of economic and social development programs. Many of the policy
recommendations, however, were based on some explicit or implicit
assumptions about the characteristics of the labor supply or the structure
of the labor market—that is, job and location preferences of the Saudi
workers; the social, economic, and information constraints on labor
mobility; or the work-time pattern of the existing Saudi and non-Saudi
labor force. Such assumptions, important as they were to the efficacy of
the various policy options, were nevertheless without adequate empirical
foundation. The Labor Market Study, on which this book is based, was
initiated to address this information gap. The importance of this information to planning efforts in Saudi Arabia derived from the concern of the
Ministry of Planning with how the high rate of capital outlays during the
late 1970s and the composition of these outlays were affecting current and
potential disparities in regional growth on the one hand, and the overall
development of Saudi human resources on the other.

Initial Concerns

One of the principal objectives of the study was to examine the labor
market in Saudi Arabia in a regional context. This involved measurement
of the regional distribution of labor at the time of the field survey
(summer 1978) and assessment of labor mobility among the kingdom's
five regions.[12] The underlying rationale was that as the pace of growth and

development varied among regions, the associated labor market adjustments were differentially manifested. Such information was crucial to guiding the requisite manpower allocations within a framework that tried to integrate regional and national development plans. Another important initial objective of the present study was to examine national and regional institutional rigidities in the labor market (such as the system of information flows, the process of skill formation, and the provision of the necessary incentives) that may reduce its capacity to adapt to the pressure of increasing capital expenditures on the demand and supply of local and foreign labor. The wealth of information generated in this study, however, enabled the authors to go beyond the initial objectives to the more general one of capturing the basic behavioral and institutional elements on both sides of a labor market in the midst of transition.

Study Design and Methodology

Conceptual formulation of the study began in October and November 1977. The broad objectives of the study were set in discussions with officials in the MOP, the Central Department of Statistics (CDS), and the regional labor office in Riyadh. In January 1978 the objectives and design of the study, as well as its main tools and methodologies, were outlined. These were revised in March 1978 on the basis of a limited pretesting exercise carried out in February 1978. To a large extent, the basic logic and spirit of the study design were maintained. The Labor Market Study was designed to collect national and regional information on the basic characteristics of the Saudi labor market. To establish trends in some variables, the questionnaires included prospective and retrospective questions. The information was derived from three separate samples: establishments in both public and private sectors (385 managers); 2,052 establishment workers; and 1,139 households. These three cross-sectional field surveys covered the kingdom's five regions.

Within this general framework the study attempted to collect information on three major aspects of the labor market in Saudi Arabia: (1) the sectoral classification of establishments and their technological and market characteristics, along with a wide range of measures of their strategies and standards in both external and internal labor markets; (2) an assessment of the critical labor market mechanisms and institutional arrangements which influence labor allocation and mobility within and among regions; and (3) the skills, experience, performance, past and intended behavior, preferences, and labor market knowledge of individuals, both currently employed and unemployed. Given this structure of information, a study design was developed subject to a number of constraints based on the scope and objectives of the study. Some of these constraints were set by the Ministry of Planning; others resulted from data limitations and other survey problems specific to Saudi conditions. The following are some of these constraints:

• The findings for the formal sector (establishments and workers) needed to be generalizable and therefore representative of the five planning regions of the kingdom (Central, Eastern, Northern, Southern,[13] and Western); broad nationality classifications (Saudis and non-Saudis), since an important objective was to examine the relationship between the supplies of these types of workers in the labor market; and public and private sectors, since it was expected that the structure of demand would be different in these two sectors.

• Information regarding nonformal employment and the extent of current unemployment had to be collected and incorporated in the analysis.

• The need to utilize the findings in the preparation of the third five-year plan (1981–85)[14] called for a tight time schedule. Given the national coverage of the study, its wide and complex analytical scope, and its composition (three separate surveys conducted in the kingdom's five regions), the time constraint was one of the most stringent. Pretesting, interviewer recruiting, training, and final preparation of these and all other field study tools were completed between January and April 1978. Field work was started in May 1978 and ended in September 1978. All documentation for analysis—coding and editing books, analysis plans, and computer programming—were completed in October 1978. Initial tabulation required for the first draft was completed in December 1978. Checking of all tables and preliminary analysis was completed in January 1979. Initial findings were sent to the MOP from November 1978 to January 1979. A draft two-volume report was submitted in February 1979; the final report, in September 1979.

• One of the main difficulties in planning a major survey study is the availability of an up-to-date sample frame. At the time of study preparation, census information was not available in a usable form. The only other available data source was that developed for the Ministry of Planning as part of a study undertaken by Coopers and Lybrand Associates, Ltd.[15] Given the resource and time constraints just mentioned, it was decided to use the Coopers and Lybrand final sample as the frame for the private establishment sample. Aside from accessibility and convenience, the use of the Coopers and Lybrand sample as the sample frame for the present study had other advantages, most important of which is that it included establishment-level data that could be used to check the consistency of our findings. For that purpose a system of cross-matching

Table 1-1. Basic Sample Information

Sample	Attempted						Completed						Final sample[a]					
	All	C	E	N	S	W	All	C	E	N	S	W	All	C	E	N	S	W
Establishments	468	146	110	20	34	158	375	110	94	14	23	134	385	107	94	14	35	134
Saudi workers	1,166	405	318	59	57	327	1,043	286	317	56	57	327	1,050	283	318	56	64	329
Non-Saudi workers	854	311	212	39	79	213	810	269	212	37	79	213	1,002	212	208	38	109	211
Households	1,000	220	210	180	180	210	1,114	227	272	187	180	248	1,139	224	266	192	181	281
Saudi													867	186	163	152	150	221
Non-Saudi													272	38	103	40	31	60

Note: Column headings indicate planning regions: C, Central; E, Eastern; N, Northern; S, Southern (more formally, Southwestern); and W, Western.

a. Because of the additional sample in the final stages of the field work, the numbers shown under the final sample are larger than what was initially designed.

Source: Unless otherwise specified, all tabular material presented in this book derives from Labor Market Study computer tape.

between the two data sets was developed and integrated in the data filing system.

• Since the study was both large and complex, it required adequately trained and supervised field workers and a considerable back-up of technical expertise. Survey experience in the kingdom was both recent and limited. A consultant, the Middle East Marketing Research Bureau, was contracted to conduct the field work and develop the initial tabulations under the technical direction and supervision of the World Bank. As part of a long-range attempt to develop research capabilities in Saudi Arabia, Saudi students from a number of universities were involved in the interviewing activities of the study.

• The initial study design gave scientific and general guidelines. Because of lack of information on the various details of the labor market—such as the proportion of Saudi workers in the various types of establishments—it was necessary to have a flexible design. For example, contrary to expectations, it was found that very few Saudis were employed in private establishments. This information became apparent only after field work was well in progress. Scientifically, it was not possible to generate, or even guess, such information from the limited pretesting exercise. The fact that Saudis are a small minority in private establishments was itself a finding of the study. Accordingly, it was decided to supplement the sample of large establishments and to interview all Saudis up to a maximum of ten in every selected establishment. The added sample was selected scientifically with known probability.

Given these constraints, a multistage stratified sample was developed to reflect the major characteristics of both supply and demand for labor. For the private establishment sample, the Coopers and Lybrand sample was divided by size (large and small) and by region (five). An added classification to reflect the level of technology was also made. Within each category a specified number of establishments was selected randomly. In the case of public establishments, a list was prepared for each region; they were then classified according to the general level of technical skills required for operation, and a sample was selected. For each selected establishment, private or public, a comprehensive list of all workers was prepared and divided into Saudi and non-Saudi workers. A sample of workers was then selected within the broad nationality classification and stratified by level of skill. Finally, an independent national sample of households stratified according to region and by urban and rural residence was developed. All heads of selected households and an additional adult male, if available, were interviewed. The final structure of the three samples is given in table 1-1.

All the study elements at the various stages were documented: overall design, sampling, interviewing schedules, coding books, and computer analysis requests. A systematic reference procedure was developed and adopted throughout to link tabulation plans, computer output, coding books, and the original questionnaires. These were necessary procedures since the information collected in this study can serve as a basic socioeconomic data bank for planning purposes beyond the present immediate use.

Organization of the Book

This book does not attempt to provide a general survey of the labor market in Saudi Arabia. Nor does it claim to be a quantitative assessment of the dynamics of that market.[16] The book instead tries to capture the essence of a labor market in transition, and attempts to identify the operative elements at both ends of the transition process: the pull of tradition and the push of modernity. Such an effort would be meaningless, however, if it were presented without the benefit of a theoretical framework for labor market operation. Chapter 2 accordingly presents two competing theories—the neoclassical theory and a cluster of segmentation theories—each of which attempts to explain the behavior of the labor market. The chapter provides a strategy of analysis in the context of the Saudi labor market that borrows from these two frameworks.

Once the notion of a market is introduced, one must explore the analysis of supply and demand. Chapter 3 aims at capturing the various aspects of labor supply: those related to demography, and those related to skill formation. Chapter 4 focuses on aspects of labor demand: economic growth and structural change at both the aggregate and the sectoral levels. The book then moves to the institutional framework of the labor market in Saudi Arabia. Organizationally, chapter 5 distinguishes between market actors (workers and employers) and market practices. The survey findings are organized to describe the behavior of the market actors, whether it be the characteristics and preferences of the workers or the benefits accruing to, expectations of, and the constraints on the employers. The market practices cover a wide range from unemployment compensation to the process of job search, the nature of contractual arrangements, and promotion opportunities.

How the Saudis responded to the changing conditions in the labor market is described systematically in the following four chapters. Chapter 6 focuses on the process of skill formation in its three dimensions: eradication of adult illiteracy, formal education, and training (on-the-job as well as off-the-job). It tries to uncover the motivating factors which prompt individuals to go through the laborious process of skill formation.

Chapter 7 concentrates on wage and family income. The information contained herein will undoubtedly shed some important light on income distribution in Saudi Arabia in 1978. Equally interesting are the wage determinants which are derived from a statistical analysis of wage and income earners classified by some seventeen variables. Elements of tradition and modernity assemble side by side to explain wage and income differentials as reported by Saudi respondents.

In response to changes sweeping through the labor market, Saudis would be expected to move from one location to another, as well as from one job to another. Chapter 8 analyzes the process of geographic mobility, in terms of past and future plans. It utilizes multivariate analysis to identify the socioeconomic variables which stimulate geographic mobility and the other variables which discourage it. Chapter 9 undertakes a similar exercise with the process of occupational mobility. Finally, chapter 10 provides a synopsis of the findings and attempts to highlight their relevance for policy formulation.

Notes

1. The present kingdom was first constituted on September 23, 1932.
2. Kingdom of Saudi Arabia, Central Planning Organization, *[First] Development Plan, 1390 AH [1970–75]* (Dammam: Al-Mutawa Press, 1970).
3. Naiem A. Sherbiny, "Sectoral Employment Projections with Minimum Data: The case of Saudi Arabia," in Naiem A. Sherbiny, ed., *Manpower Planning in the Oil Countries*, supplement 1 to *Research in Human Capital and Development: A Research Annual* (Greenwich, Conn.: JAI Press, 1981), pp. 173–206.
4. Kingdom of Saudi Arabia, Central Planning Organization, *[Second] Development Plan, 1395–1400 AH [1975–80]* (Riyadh: Ministry of Planning 1975).
5. Kingdom of Saudi Arabia, Saudi Arabian Monetary Agency, Research and Statistics Department, *Annual Report, 1400* (Riyadh, December 1980).
6. See, for example, Naiem A. Sherbiny and Ismail Serageldin, "Expatriate Labor and Economic Growth: Saudi Demand for Egyptian Labor," in *Rich and Poor States in the Middle East: Egypt and the New Arab Order*, Malcom H. Kerr and El Sayed Yassin, eds. (Boulder, Colo.: Westview Press; Cairo, Egypt: American University in Cairo Press, 1982), pp. 225–57.
7. World Bank estimate based on Saudi data.
8. Numerous publications have attempted to assess the origins and overall impact of the rapid Saudi development process, a task much wider than that represented by the present volume. Relevant volumes include Faisal S. Al-Bashir, *A Structural Econometric Model of the Saudi Arabian Economy, 1960–1970* (New York: Ronald Press, 1977); Fouad Al-Farsy, *Saudi Arabia: A Case Study in Development* (London and Boston: Kegan Paul International, 1982); Robert E. Looney, *Saudi Arabia's Development Potential: Application of an Islamic Growth Model* (Lexington, Mass.: Lexington Books, 1981); Ragaei El-Mallakh,

Saudi Arabia: Rush to Development (Baltimore, Md.: Johns Hopkins University Press, 1982); and Arthur N. Young, *Saudi Arabia: The Making of a Financial Giant*, Near Eastern Civilization Studies no. 8 (New York: New York University Press, 1983). On the role of the Bedouin, see D. P. Cole, "Bedouin and Social Change in Saudi Arabia," *Journal of Asian and African Studies*, vol. 16 (January-April 1981), pp. 128–49.

9. For the legal background in the early 1970s, see U.S. Department of Labor, Bureau of Labor Statistics, *Labor Law and Practice in the Kingdom of Saudi Arabia*, BLS Report no. 407 (Washington, D.C.: U.S. Government Printing Office, 1973); for the situation a decade later, see Q. Favid Mian and Alison Lerrick, *Saudi Business and Labour Law: Its Interpretation and Application* (London: Graham and Trotman, 1982). See also N. H. Kanam, tr., *Business Laws of Saudi Arabia*, 2 vols. (London: Graham and Trotman, 1980).

10. *Development Plan, 1395–1400AH [1975–80]*, pp. 213–368.

11. For further details on model development, see Ismail Serageldin and Bob Li, *Tools for Manpower Planning: The World Bank Models*: vol. 1, *Technical Presentation of the Models*; vol. 2, *User's Guide for the Country (Compound) Model*; vol. 3, *User's Guide for the Regional (Expanded) Model*; and vol. 4, *User's Guide for the Migration Model*, World Bank Staff Working Papers, nos. 587–90 (Washington, D.C., May 1983). These publications complement Ismail Serageldin, James A. Socknat, Stace Birks, Bob Li, and Clive A. Sinclair, *Manpower and International Labor Migration in the Middle East and North Africa* (New York: Oxford University Press, 1983).

12. For planning purposes, the five regions are the Central, Eastern, Northern, Southern, and Western. They are to be distinguished from the eighteen provinces (six major, twelve minor) of the kingdom, which are administrative entities, and also from the fourteen subregional divisions combining districts used in census enumeration.

13. Throughout this book, the common use of the term "Southern region" or "South" and the formal use of the term "Southwestern region" refer to the same entity.

14. Kingdom of Saudi Arabia, Ministry of Planning, *Third Development Plan, 1400–1405 AH, 1980–1985 AD* (Riyadh, 1980).

15. *Outline Functional Specification of a Macroeconomic Model for Saudi Arabia* (Riyadh: Ministry of Planning, April 1977).

16. An ancillary effort was subsequently undertaken through a field study as part of the manpower development consulting agreement between the Royal Commission for Jubail and Yanbu and the Korean Development Institute, subsequently published as Linsu Kim, *Motivation Survey in Saudi Arabia* (Seoul: Korean Development Institute, 1980).

2. Conceptual Considerations: A Survey of Basic Issues

In GENERAL, SOCIOECONOMIC PLANNING in Saudi Arabia has been conceived as the instrument to transform a traditional society into a modern industrial one. This is being done in a relatively short time and in the context of free competition in production and exchange that provides adequate incentives for the growth of private business activities, private initiative, and employment. The development process involves two major resource constraints: financial and human. As indicated in chapter 1, Saudi Arabia in the mid-1960s shared the financial constraint with the majority of developing countries; it was not until the early 1970s that human resources (including skills) became the binding constraint to accelerated development. The quantity and quality of available manpower resources accordingly emerged as the main factors limiting rapid economic development.

Central to this process of accelerated human resource development in Saudi Arabia is a labor market that is both adaptable and efficient in allocating the supply of labor among various occupations and between different locations, as well as in determining wage rates. This chapter examines briefly the various theories underlying the operation of the labor market, their applicability to the situation in Saudi Arabia, and their role as a framework for the empirical analysis in this book.

Theories of Labor Market Behavior

There are two main streams of thought in the analysis of labor market behavior: the neoclassical or orthodox theory and the segmented labor market theories.[1] In general, the neoclassical model is based on the fundamental marginal theory: a profit-maximizing behavior of employers in determining their demand for labor, and utility maximization behavior of workers in developing their skill levels (human capital formation) and making choices between leisure and work hours. The various segmented labor market theories take issue with many of the theoretical, empirical, and policy implications of the neoclassical model; they give more emphasis to the structural properties of the labor market relative to the behavioral elements of workers and employers as a basic determinant of the functioning of the labor market. This section outlines the two competing theories and examines their main tenets. It concludes with a strategy of analysis that borrows from the two theoretical frameworks.

The Neoclassical Model

Whether the discussion concerns a commodity or a service, the orthodox theory stipulates the existence of a "market" in which the forces of demand and supply interact to determine how much of the commodity or service is exchanged and at what price. Labor services are no exception, where the market mechanism determines the number employed and the wage level. The labor market is thus a vehicle through which businessmen (demand) and workers (supply) interact to determine the size and allocation of work effort and the wage rates acceptable to both sides. The theory abstracts the behavior of the agents (actors) in a model form and defines the rules and mechanism of the market.

The neoclassical model assumes perfect competition where, in equilibrium, all jobs are viewed by workers as equivalent and all workers are viewed by employers as a homogeneous entity. Workers make choices to maximize their satisfaction. They will continue to invest in improving their skills as long as the present value of the benefit of such an investment exceeds its cost. Essentially, workers will trade income for effort until the satisfaction of an added unit of income is at least equal to that of a unit of leisure time. These tradeoffs may also include the assessment of costs and benefits which are not strictly pecuniary. Employers, however, are seen as offering jobs to maximize profits. The governing rule in the individual firm is the marginal revenue productivity of labor.

Under conditions of perfect competition, the labor market is assumed to operate continuously, producing uninterrupted flows of labor services at appropriate prices. The market efficiently matches jobs and potential workers. Within this framework, individuals try to move from low- to high-income areas and from low- to high-paying jobs. Workers are postulated to invest in their own skills until the costs and returns of such investments are equalized at the margin.

The theory does not imply that such ideal conditions are the way of life. It recognizes that discontinuity may arise—for example, there may be noncompeting groups, a shortage of labor in some geographic areas and an abundance in others, or persistent job vacancies in an industry or enterprise. In the neoclassical framework these cases are presumed to result from operating factors outside the postulated behavior of the market. The implied policy response, accordingly, is to try to ensure "fluidity" to the labor market: to restore the conditions that, it is assumed, will bring perfect competition. The theory, however, fails to explain why these "imperfections" arise in the first place. It is the inability of the neoclassical theory to explain some of the observed phenomena and outcomes of the labor market, which are neither economically optimal nor socially desirable, that prompted the challenge of segmentation theories as an alternative framework.

Segmentation Theories

There is no single theory of segmented labor markets,[2] but a general dissatisfaction with the lack of adequate explanations of various outcomes of the labor market. A list would include the persistence of poverty (and unemployment) in the midst of affluence, the apparent failure of education and training programs to reduce inequalities in income and in the acquisition of human skills, hiring practices of employers that are at variance with the assumed rationality of maximizing behavior, and discrimination. A common theme among segmentation theorists, however, is that "a particular structuring of the labor market 'segmentation' defined as a *structural form of relationship* can be revealed between individuals as a whole and jobs as a whole. The next step is to identify the form of this structuring and at the same time the mechanisms which account for it. This of course means that such mechanisms must be sought within the actual functioning of the labor market, i.e., that the phenomenon of segmentation is considered as *endogenous* to the labor market."[3]

The job competition theory, one variant of the segmentation theories, is an attempt to make endogenous some structural properties of the labor market.[4] Its main elements are that the number and types of jobs available are determined by the prevailing technology and that social customs and institutions are more important factors than workers' skills and the wages they accept in determining the number and types of jobs actually filled. Furthermore, wages are not flexible downward as implied by the assumed smooth operation of the market. In addition, some intrafirm decisions (such as those regarding promotions and on-the-job training) are relatively insulated from the mechanics of the market, even though they are directly relevant to labor market operation. When such key allocative decisions are made within firms, a significant part of job allocation is demand oriented. Accordingly, observable human capital characteristics appear to be downgraded as significant determinants of wage levels.

A Proposed Strategy for Analysis

The proponents of these two paradigms, the neoclassical and the segmented market theories, seem to make unnecessarily extreme efforts to illustrate differences rather than common grounds in their positions.[5] However, it seems that these theories could be viewed more as complements than as substitutes. Both paradigms could be utilized in a complementary fashion to guide the analysis of the labor market, especially when the structural parameters for the market are rapidly changing and/or the competitive nature of the market is being encouraged— probably characteristics of the Saudi labor market at present. In attempting to assess the number of employed workers and understand the process of wage determination in the Saudi market, the neoclassical paradigm may be used as a guide which abstracts from the fine details on either the supply or demand sides and works with labor as if it were homogeneous. Under the assumptions of perfect competition and mobility, the resultant solutions are also economically efficient. When attention is paid to the finer details, however, the labor market picture becomes clouded, crowded, or even confused. The following section attempts to explore the main structural forces in the labor market that justify the use of two competing theoretical frameworks. This is followed by a discussion of some basic characteristics of the Saudi labor market and an attempt to develop hypotheses regarding the pattern of workers' response to the changing environment by drawing from the two competing paradigms.

Specific Issues in Labor Market Analysis

There are unsettled issues related to the homogeneity of labor, to its spatial and temporal allocation, and to the process of wage determination that need careful assessment. It is in these areas that segmentation theories may provide the proper context for the analysis of the Saudi labor market.

Labor Homogeneity

A priori, labor is not a homogeneous entity. There are separate functions for the demand and supply not only of broad categories of labor (skilled, semiskilled, unskilled), but also—more important—of special- ized categories (managers, professionals, farmers, sales workers, and so on) or even subcategories (such as doctors, engineers, accountants). In fact, in modern economies the classification goes to a much finer level of detail (mechanical, electrical, and civil engineers). Soon we no longer have a single labor market but a whole set of skill markets. In large and widespread economies the spatial dimension becomes an integral factor determining the outcome of market behavior. Thus there are no longer markets for specific skills but skill-specific markets in various locations.

The labor market is therefore a complex matrix of individual special- ized markets in various locations. Accordingly, wage rates do not emerge as a single value from the equilibrium solution but as a range or band. In short, the labor market is simply the aggregation of individual markets (by skill and location) which, by nature or practice, are segmented. Under these conditions it is not surprising that skeptics would question the validity of empirically analyzing the labor market or, for that matter, the very existence of the labor market. The issue, however, remains whether these submarkets can be analyzed within a neoclassical framework. The degree of labor mobility between such markets, that is, their "permeability," is relevant in assessing the severity of the segmenta- tion.

Labor Mobility

Labor mobility is an essential attribute of a well-functioning labor market. For example, the interconnections between the local and na- tional labor markets come from imbalances in supply and demand at the local level, which are compensated by geographic mobility at the national level. Conceptually, markets with an excess supply of a particular skill will push labor out to other local markets in which there is an excess demand. The opposite is also true: local markets with an excess demand for a specific skill are expected to attract labor from other markets with an excess supply of such skill. As an aggregation of local markets, the national market may show a balance for a particular skill or group of skills. However, the differential spatial distribution of demand and sup- ply may induce labor mobility between localities. Although such mobility may be induced in part by wage differentials, it seems to be induced largely by variant employment opportunities; these in turn are explained by differences in the economic growth of localities and the operation of the market mechanism in local labor markets. How much mobility will occur, under what inducement, and to what distance will also depend on social and individual characteristics. The final outcome can only be taken as a postulate subject to empirical testing and verification.

Market Segmentation and Occupational Mobility

The relations between the specialized labor markets are less clear. In general, it appears that imbalances in supply and demand in one specialized labor market may have little or nothing to do with the next specialized market—at least in the short run, though it is likely to be less true in the long run. Because labor supply responds with a lag to market signals, specialized labor markets are separate and separable in the short run; once enough time has elapsed to allow for the lag in supply response, they are no longer separate. Since higher skills take longer to acquire, the lag in supply response will be longer.

Eventually, the specialized markets are interconnected *at the margin*. If at some point, for example, there is an excess supply of engineers and an excess demand for medical doctors, nothing can be done in the short run to get engineers to perform the physicians' job. Engineers' wages will be depressed relative to physicians' wages, and some engineers will remain unemployed until demand catches up with the *existing* supply at some future point. However, such conditions are strong signals which affect the decisions of new entrants to college. Fewer students will be entering engineering schools; more will go to medical schools. Thus, the supply of specialized skills, while responding to market signals, seems perpetually to lag behind these signals. When viewed as a dynamic process, a balance of supply and demand is likely to be the rare exception.

Perhaps this is a dramatization of another function of the labor market, that of occupational mobility. The lower the level of specialized skills, the easier it is for the worker to move from one occupation to the next. For example, clerks are easily trained to be sales workers and vice versa, but it is not so easy for specialized engineers to swap jobs. And it would take years of re-education and retraining before an engineer could perform a physician's job or vice versa. The type of occupational mobility most commonly observed through the operation of the labor market is the promotion from lower to higher levels within the same line of activity. Clerks become minor administrators, professionals become managers, and so on. In such cases, experience and on-the-job training become decisive in occupational mobility.

Wage Determination

As the previous discussion illustrates, an important function of the labor market is to provide timely and accurate signals for both supply and demand sides to adjust wages in disequilibrium situations. Under optimal conditions, these induced adjustments should lead to the most efficient allocative decisions. For example, the presence of an excess supply of a particular skill will tend to depress real wages and benefits for these particular skills relative to those of other skills. These real wage changes act as signals to employers and skilled workers alike. Employers are tempted, other things being equal, to employ more of these skill-specific workers at lower relative wages. When wage rates tend to be relatively inflexible, as in the case of professionals and organized labor, unemployment, not wage reduction, then becomes the market signal. On the supply side, potential suppliers of skills tend to acquire the particular skills with the generally higher expected net gain. The expected net gain is equal to the expected real wage minus the expected cost of acquiring the specific skill. Accordingly, the structure of wages provides the signals for the functioning of the labor market.

Wage determination, on the other hand, is a corollary result of the operation of the labor market and the interaction of the forces of labor supply and demand. As already indicated, given the structure of labor market segmentation and the possible institutional rigidity of wage levels, there is no reason to expect that the resultant structure of wages is necessarily optimal. But the very forces that shape the structure of wages are those that induce geographic or occupational mobility. For this reason an empirical examination of any one of those processes must also take the other two into account. Some of these joint effects could be captured within a multivariate analysis framework. A more complete analysis would be to specify a simultaneous equation system which captures geographic mobility, occupational mobility, and wage determination as endogenous variables. An analysis of wage determination should at least start with providing information on whether wages are partly determined by relative skill levels, whether there exist differences among and within sectors (public and private), and whether there are differences by occupational groups. This type of information provides the essential base for a policy-oriented analysis of the labor market, but does not require a full specification of that market.

The Saudi Labor Market: Main Issues

To what extent does the preceding theoretical discussion provide guidelines for the analysis of our central question: How does the Saudi work force adjust to this rapidly changing environment? To do so, some unique characteristics of the Saudi labor market need first to be examined.

Although the Saudi labor market has much in common with other labor markets in developing countries, it also has some unique features: a large inflow of expatriate labor, a significant nomadic population, a massive training program, a relatively large area and a relatively dispersed population, and minimal institutional rigidities in the functioning of the market. The first three factors warrant special elaboration.

Expatriate Labor

Expatriates make up a large and increasing portion of the employed work force: from about 27 percent in 1970, they have expanded to 40 percent in 1975, and about 53 percent in 1980. They have crossed international borders to the Saudi labor market in response to the country's large demand for labor which far exceeded the local supply. This excess demand for labor created significant shortages in a wide variety of skills, which have resulted in substantially higher wage rates in Saudi Arabia than in many neighboring Arab and Asian countries. For these reasons, expatriates are spread across all skill levels and in all regions of the country. Literally hundreds of thousands of unskilled and semiskilled expatriate workers are employed throughout the five regions of Saudi Arabia.

This massive inflow of foreign labor has important conceptual implications both for the functioning of the market and for the development of Saudi labor. Expatriate labor is expected to reduce imbalances in supply and demand in the various segments of the market. This may tend to speed the adjustment mechanism. Alternatively, it may reduce the mobility of the Saudi workers since the incentives, in terms of wage (and benefit) differentials, are being reduced. In addition, competition from foreign skilled workers may make it less attractive for Saudi workers to acquire new skills or may cause Saudi workers to disassociate themselves altogether from certain professions, such as construction and sanitary services. As a result, new attitudes may develop, and Saudis already in the labor force or potentially entering it may consider certain jobs and professions as desirable, others as undesirable. These are relevant and empirically testable policy issues.

The Nomadic Population

The nomadic population in Saudi Arabia is generally understood to constitute a significant proportion of the total population and the labor force. No recent official figures are available, and widely variant estimates range from a high of 3 million in the early 1930s by an individual researcher to a low of 700,000 in 1962 by the Saudi government.[6] Only the fourteen district volumes of the 1974 census have been released, not the overall volume summarizing and aggregating district results. Even research attempts that addressed the issue of population and labor in Saudi Arabia and went to the length of deriving some figures for the national level by aggregating district results, though a commendable effort, could not produce consistent estimates of the nomadic population.[7] This ambiguity surrounding nomadic population and labor undoubtedly impedes a full analysis of the implications of these variables for the operation of the Saudi labor market. Only a tentative analysis can be made as to how, and through what mechanism, this inadequately defined portion of the population will be integrated in the mainstream of the labor force. Specifically, demand-oriented policies that attempt to increase the employment of nomads through increases in generalized expenditures will have an entirely different impact on the functioning of the labor market from supply-oriented policies that focus on training and incentives to mobility, such as sedenterization schemes and summer training campaigns.

Labor Training Programs

Another unique feature of the Saudi labor market is the massive program to train Saudis employed in a wide range of occupations and activities. The rationale for this phenomenon comes from the proclaimed policy of Saudi authorities to "Saudize" the decisionmaking functions at practically all levels of government. There is, however, no adequate empirical knowledge about the extent of Saudization in the public sector. Many Saudis who are less than trained or prepared to take over managerial or administrative functions in the government or public sector may find themselves given such responsibilities in the hope that they will become trained on the job. In fact, many succeed in doing so admirably. In addition to this on-the-job training, extensive formal programs are available to improve the technical and managerial capabilities of the staff.

A Strategy for Analysis

Although this analysis examines the Saudi labor market and its operation in general, a special effort addresses the development of the Saudi work force from three major perspectives: supply, demand, and the role of institutional and structural factors in such development. On the basis of the theoretical discussion and the special characteristics of the Saudi labor market, an analytical framework is formulated, as shown below, for each perspective.

Supply Factors

Conceptually, the supply of labor may be viewed as partly exogenous and partly endogenous, determined simultaneously with the growth and structure of economic activities, that is, the supply of job opportunities.

Endogenously, labor supply is determined by the size of the potential work force and participation rates. The size of the Saudi component of the potential work force could be viewed as exogenous, given prevailing mortality levels, at least for the next fifteen years, since new entrants to the labor force during this period are already born. In contrast, participation rates, in terms of both decisions to join the labor force and hours of work, are more sensitive to short-term socioeconomic conditions. In Saudi Arabia, the demand for labor in almost all skill and occupational levels has been quite strong since the early 1970s. The question is: What is the supply response? Theoretically, within a human capital framework, Saudis will increase their labor force participation if the demand for their services increases, since it is most certain to be associated with an increase in wages, at least in the short run. There would be geographic mobility as workers move from areas with low demand to areas with high demand. The value of additional training to acquire new skills in greater demand should be reflected in an increased demand for training by potential and existing workers. This is basically the neoclassical framework that envisages a smooth continuity in the allocative function of the labor market. The segmentation theories provide some cautionary provisos.

An important assumption of the neoclassical paradigm is perfect, or at least equal, access to information regarding job openings. However, there is no reason to expect that knowledge about available opportunities is equally widespread among job seekers, or that the cost of search for these job alternatives is not prohibitive for many workers. Accordingly, mobility is reduced because of factors beyond workers' control. Improving the market information network should minimize such imperfections. It is also possible that the geographic mobility of Saudis in the labor force, or their occupational choices, are controlled more by noneconomic factors, such as values and attitudes, which may not be easily influenced by policy. Most important, the Saudi labor market is not a closed system. It is not limited to Saudis, but extends to a much larger universe that provides an essentially unlimited supply. Accordingly, there is no reason to assume a priori that the market will provide price signals to the Saudi component. With few exceptions, such as key administrative or other sensitive occupations for which only Saudi nationals would be eligible, shortages, regional or occupational, could be filled in relatively short order from abroad. Interregional and interoccupational wage differentials may be dampened; thus the extent of mobility and the demand for training by the Saudi component of the labor force may be less than expected. This pattern of expatriate-national labor substitution is a structural characteristic of the Saudi labor market. An analytic framework to test Saudi labor responsiveness to these new opportunities should include both the main price forces underlying the neoclassical paradigm and the structural forces indicated by the segmentation theories.

Demand Factors

It is established that the demand for labor is derived from the demand for goods and services. Changes in the latter sooner or later produce changes in the former. As a result, demand for labor in Saudi Arabia during the 1970s increased in line with the continuously rising demand for goods and services. Underlying such a relationship is the concept of a production function. Although no specification of a production function for the Saudi economy is attempted, the concept unquestionably defines the basis of the relationship between gross domestic product (GDP) and employment, both in the national economy and at the sectoral level.

In the analysis of labor demand, a particular use will be made of the concept of "patterns of growth," initially identified by Kuznets. It was demonstrated that as per capita GDP grows, the sectoral composition of GDP changes over time in a systematic pattern derived from several historic experiences. The shares in GDP of primary sectors fall, those of secondary sectors rise, and those of tertiary sectors generally remain stable. The notion of patterns of growth was extended by Chenery to the structure of employment and generalized to the experiences of developing countries.[8]

In testing the patterns of growth hypothesis in Saudi Arabia, the hypothesis received general support, as will be detailed in chapter 4. In summary, the rapid growth of per capita GDP during the 1970s was accompanied by rapid expansion in employment. Of course, the relative shares of the individual sectors in output and employment did not follow the Chenery blueprint—generally because of the unique features which distinguish the Saudi economy. These include the special role accorded the development of human resources in government expenditures, and the special effort to encourage private initiative despite the increased role of the public sector in the national economy.

There are additional factors beyond the level of GDP which determine the demand for labor. At the national level the wage rate enters as a determinant. This ensures that the relation between marginal productivity of labor and the prevailing wage rate is not violated. At some sectoral levels of disaggregation, the rate of technical progress must be included in the determinants of demand for labor. If technology is defined as a specification of a capital-labor ratio, biased technical progress (non-neutral) must, by definition, tend to alter the prevailing capital-labor ratios at the margin, and hence change the coefficients of capital and labor with respect to output. Thus, for given increments in output, changes in technology must, by definition, affect the rates of change in the demand for capital and labor. Changes in technology may occur discretely—for example, in the way resources are organized and combined in the production process—and may also be embodied in machinery and equipment that raise labor productivity in more than one way: by outperforming old machines, devising new approaches to existing problems, or developing new processes that bypass established processes.

Market Institutions

Some of the institutional arrangements in the labor market of Saudi Arabia are common in other developing countries; examples are the absence of a formal process of collective bargaining and the prevalence of informality in hiring practices. Other institutional factors are shaped by *Shari'a* (Islamic law), as detailed in labor and wage legislation. The guiding principle is that workers' well-being is the responsibility of the state. The large inflows of expatriate workers, however, are creating needs to form new institutions or to develop existing ones to cope with an increasingly complex environment of the labor market.

Notes

1. See, for example, the review by Glen G. Cain, "The Challenge of Segmented Labor Market Theories to Orthodox Theory: A Survey," *Journal of Economic Literature*, vol. 14, no. 4 (December 1976), pp. 1215-57; and two companion volumes issued by the Organisation for Economic Co-operation and Development (OECD), *Structural Determinants of Employment and Unemployment* (Paris: OECD, vol. 1, 1977; vol. 2, 1979). Other relevant discussions may be found in Paul Binoch, *Urban Unemployment in Developing Countries* (Geneva: International Labour Office, 1973); James M. Buchanan, *The Bases for Collective Action* (New York: General Learning Press, 1971); M. J. Carter, "Competition and Segmentation in Internal Labor Markets," *Journal of Economic Issues*, vol. 16 (December 1982), pp. 1063-77; H. B. Chenery and M. Syrquin, *Patterns of Development, 1950-1970*

(London: Oxford University Press, 1975); Edgar C. Edwards, ed., *Employment in Developing Nations* (New York: Columbia University Press, 1974); William Fellner, *The Economics of Technological Advance* (New York: General Learning Press, 1971); Gary S. Fields, *How Segmented Is the Bogotá Labor Market?* World Bank Staff Working Paper no. 434 (Washington, D.C., 1980); Suzan Horton and Timothy King, *Labor Productivity: Un Tour d'Horizon*, World Bank Staff Working Paper no. 497 (Washington, D.C., 1981); International Labour Organization (ILO), *Manpower and Employment in Arab Countries: Some Critical Issues* (Geneva: ILO, 1975); Simon Kuznets, *Modern Economic Growth* (New Haven, Conn.: Yale University Press, 1965); Dipak Mazumdar, *The Urban Labor Market and Income Distribution: A Study of Malaysia* (New York: Oxford University Press, 1981); Dipak Mazumdar, *Paradigms in the Study of Urban Labor Markets in LDCs: A Reassessment in the Light of an Empirical Study in Bombay City*, World Bank Staff Working Paper no. 336 (Washington, D.C., 1979); Orville John McDiarmid, *Unskilled Labor for Development: Its Economic Cost* (Baltimore, Md.: Johns Hopkins University Press, 1977); Rakesh Mohan, *The Determinants of Labour Earnings in Developing Metropoli: Estimates from Bogotá and Cali, Colombia*, World Bank Staff Working Paper no. 498 (Washington, D.C., 1981); Gerald L. Nordquist, *The Behavior of Competitive Enterprises: Theory, Application, and Performance* (Morristown, N.J.: General Learning Press, 1972); OECD, *Occupational and Educational Structures of the Labor Force and Levels of Economic Development* (Paris: OECD, 1971); M. J. Piore, "Labor Market Segmentation Theory: Critics Should Let Paradigm Evolve," *Monthly Labor Review*, vol. 106 (April 1983), pp. 26–28; G. G. Somers and W. D. Wood, eds., *Cost-Benefit Analysis of Manpower Policies* (Ontario: Hanson and Edgar, 1969); Lyn Squire, *Employment Policy in Development Countries: A Survey of Issues and Evidence* (New York: Oxford University Press, 1981); Lyn Squire, *Labor Force, Employment and Labor Markets in the Course of Economic Development*, World Bank Staff Working Paper no. 336 (Washington, D.C., 1979); and David Turnham, *The Employment Problem in Less Developed Countries* (Paris: OECD, 1971).

2. Cain, "The Challenge of Segmented Labor Market Theories"; Fields, *How Segmented Is the Bogotá Labor Market?*; R. Leroy, "Comments on the Report by G. G. Cain," in OECD, *Structural Determinants of Employment and Unemployment*, vol. 2; and Mazumdar, *Paradigms in the Study of Urban Labor Markets*.

3. Bernard Meriaux, "Employment Policies and Labor Market Theories," in OECD, *Structural Determinants of Employment and Unemployment*, vol. 2.

4. Lester C. Thurow, *The American Distribution of Income: A Structural Problem*, Joint Economic Committee, 92nd Congress, 2nd session (Washington, D.C.: U.S. Government Printing Office, 1972).

5. See, for example, Cain, "The Challenge of Segmented Labor Market Theories"; and Meriaux, "Employment Policies and Labor Market Theories."

6. The high figure reported for the early 1930s is by F. Hamza, *The Heart of Arabia* (London, 1933), as quoted in J. Stace Birks and Clive A. Sinclair, *The Kingdom of Saudi Arabia and the Libyan Arab Jamahiriya: The Key Countries of Employment*, World Employment Program Research Working Paper, WEP 2-26/WP-39 (Geneva: ILO, May 1979); and the low figure for 1962 is by the Central Department of Statistics, *Hasr al Sukkan wal Mu'assasat, 1382 AH* (Riyadh, 1963).

7. Birks and Sinclair, *The Kingdom of Saudi Arabia*.

8. Chenery and Syrquin, *Patterns of Development*; Kuznets, *Modern Economic Growth*.

3. Labor Supply and Its Dynamics

IN DESCRIBING THE FACTORS influencing labor supply, precise definition of the concept itself is necessary to avoid ambiguity. The problem of definition is particularly difficult in this area because borderline cases arise continuously. Several different definitions of "economically active population" are in use. Sometimes the concept is used to signify a particular segment of the population (usually those aged 15 to 64), to which a participation rate is then applied to define the labor force, which includes all those employed and the unemployed seeking employment. Thus the concept of labor supply, also defined as labor force, encompasses both of those categories; that is, it means the total number of persons who want employment, whether or not their wish is satisfied. The two basic components of that concept of labor force are (1) size and structure, and (2) participation or activity rates.

As a measure of the quantity of labor supply, the number of persons in the labor force is only a first approximation. A more satisfactory measure requires more refined specifications of activity rates; for example, the length of the working week, part-time or seasonal work, and the annual turnover of persons entering and leaving the labor force. Demographic factors, such as size, age, structure, and sex ratio of the total population, and the prevailing levels and trends in fertility, mortality, and migration have a direct and mostly predictable influence on the size and structure of the labor force. It also affects activity rates indirectly. With the exception of migration, however, these demographic factors have an important influence only in the long run, that is, ten or more years. In the short term, the size and structure of the labor force are usually considered exogenous factors in the analysis of the labor market.

Changes in activity rates are brought about by a whole range of economic and social factors such as educational and training levels, trends in school enrollment, the growth of the urban population, and, in the case of women, marriage and fertility patterns. Change in activity rates is thus viewed as an endogenous factor determined simultaneously with the growth and structure of economic activities, that is, the supply of job opportunities. To ascertain the degree to which all these factors influence the activity rates of the population is a complex task. The discussion in this chapter will focus mainly on the demographic factors determining the quantitative aspects of labor supply. The skill content, however, is even more significant than the size of the labor force, especially in a society experiencing socioeconomic and technological changes as dramatic as those in Saudi Arabia. In addition to the strictly demographic characteristics of the labor force, the education, skills, experience, health, and motivation of workers are among the primary determinants of the productive capacity and growth of the economy. Although all of these qualitative factors are important for an adequate assessment of the labor force, the discussion here is of the two basic components of skill formation: literacy and education (including training).

Major Demographic Features of the Labor Force

The demographic information available on Saudi Arabia is limited. The first population and housing census was conducted in 1962–63, but was considered incomplete by the government. The second was conducted in 1974–75, and although it is considered more complete, there are indications of defects in the accuracy and reliability of some of the data.[1] In addition to the national censuses, Saudi Arabia registers vital statistics, but the system has limited utility in the calculation of demographic estimates because of incomplete coverage. Accordingly, many of the demographic figures provided below are rough estimates. Four demographic features will be examined in this section: population size, population growth, age distribution, and spatial distribution.

As the population size is examined, a useful distinction will be made between Saudi and expatriate population. Although the non-Saudi population during the 1950s was rather small, it became relatively large in the 1970s and will most likely continue to grow in absolute and relative terms in the early 1980s. For this reason, future changes in labor supply in Saudi Arabia will come from two sources: Saudi population and expatriate population.

The nomadic population is another variable unique to the Saudi context that has significance for the analysis of labor supply. In traditional analysis, the typical sources of labor are surplus rural labor and urban labor. The theory of dual development is predicated on this assumption.

In the context of Saudi Arabia, however, a third source, the nomads, must be taken into account. Their role, past and present, will be examined to ascertain their potential as a future source of labor.

Population Size and Growth

The information available on the population of Saudi Arabia does not help establish a consistent frame of reference over time.[2] In the mid-1930s the total population of Saudi Arabia was estimated at about 2 million; about half rural, more than a quarter nomadic, and the rest urban.[3] Current estimates and reported figures are particularly perplexing when that early estimate and the two censuses of 1962–63 and 1974 are juxtaposed. In the first census the Saudi population was reported to be 3.30 million; no reference was made to expatriates. In the second census the Saudi population was reported to be 5.94 million and the expatriate population, 0.79 million. If both sets of figures are reasonably accurate, they would imply a growth of 5 percent for the Saudi population—a rate that has prompted independent researchers to evaluate available evidence critically. The thrust of the argument is that both figures cannot be simultaneously reliable: either the earlier figure underestimated the Saudi population or the later figure overestimated it. If the 1974 figure was accurate, Saudi population in 1962–63 should have been about 4.26 million, and the reported figure of 3.30 million would have been a serious underestimation of about 30 percent.

Two attempts were made to reconcile these figures. The first assumes that the early population estimate of 1932–33 by McGregor was reasonably accurate. Assuming an average annual rate of population growth of 2.4 percent gives a proposed estimate for 1962–63 of about 4.1 million people as compared with the 3.3 million official estimate. If this proposed estimate had been growing thereafter by an average of 2.8 percent a year, the 1974 estimate would be 5.52 million, which is still below the official figure of 5.94 million but considerably closer to it. The United Nations Economic Commission for West Asia (ECWA) followed this procedure but seems to have applied a higher rate of growth during the early period and a lower one during the intercensus period. Their estimate for 1962–63 was 5.0 million, without correcting the 1974 estimate.[4]

A second attempt to reconcile these population figures utilizes employment figures and applies some reasonable participation rates. For example, total employment figures in 1963 based on two official sources, private estimates of expatriate employment, and estimates of crude participation rates prevailing in the recent and more distant past in neighboring countries of similar cultural and ethnic makeup suggest that the Saudi population in 1963 was about 3.31 million.[5] If the 1963 estimates of Saudi employment and crude participation rates are accepted, then the reported figure of 3.30 million could be accepted as a reasonably accurate estimate of the Saudi population. This method, however, is highly sensitive to variations in the postulated crude participation rates. Special care must therefore be exercised when using such a method.

If we accept the 1962–63 population estimate and an average growth rate of Saudi population during 1963–74 of 2.8 percent a year, then the resultant figure for the Saudis in 1974 would have been 4.61 million, and the 1974 figure of 5.94 million would appear to be an overestimation. Indeed, some observers argue that the 1974 census was not based on complete enumeration, but on a sizable sample enlarged by what may have been an upwardly biased multiplier.[6]

On balance, the authors believe that most probably the 1962–63 census was an underestimate while the 1974 figure may have been somewhat overestimated. The true figures are most likely to fall within the range of these two corrections, and authors' estimates reported in table 3-1 reflect this likelihood.

Compounding the complexity of this rather uncertain demographic picture are the difficulties encountered in estimating two major components in the population of Saudi Arabia. The first is the size of the nomadic population; the second is the size of the expatriate population. It is curious to note that most formal estimates tended to be upwardly biased for nomads and downwardly biased for expatriates.

No recent official figures are available for the nomadic population. As noted in chapter 2, only widely variant estimates have circulated, and they range from a high of 3 million in the early 1930s by an individual researcher to a low of 700,000 in 1962 by the government. Even the latter is believed to be upwardly biased. Since the summary of the regional results of the 1974 census was not released, the present authors had to depend on earlier attempts by others to summarize the fourteen regional volumes. In these secondary sources, one estimate of the nomadic population was 1.88 million, out of a total population of 7.01 million.[7] It appears that such an estimate is upwardly biased. Precisely because of the inherent difficulty of making reliable estimates of the nomads, there is no way to prove or disprove one's point. The estimates of nomads in table 3-1 are only notional figures. These are at best informed guesses by the authors, and are provided merely to complete the demographic picture. Nomadic populations are believed not to have exceeded 0.5 million during the past twenty years. Furthermore, it can be argued persuasively that the substantial changes which swept the Saudi economy, particularly during the 1970s, must have drawn much of the nomadic labor to urban

Table 3-1. *Estimates of Population and Work Force*

Item	Estimates (thousands of persons)				Implied growth rate (percent)		
	1963	1970	1975	1980	1963–70	1970–75	1975–80
Population							
Total	3,600	4,770	6,080	7,940	4.1	5.0	5.5
Saudi	3,350	4,090	4,740	5,490	2.9	3.0	3.0
Nomads	478	495	422	302	0.5	−6.3	−6.5
Expatriate	250	680	1,340	2,450	15.4	14.5	12.8
Work force							
Total	815.0	1,187.3	1,679.2	2,525.0	5.5	7.2	8.5
Saudi	700.0	867.3	1,010.7	1,178.0	3.1	3.1	3.1
Expatriate	115.0	320.0	668.5	1,347.0	15.7	15.9	15.0
Crude participation rates							
Saudi	0.209	0.212	0.213	0.215			
Expatriate	0.450	0.470	0.500	0.550			
Expatriate ratios							
In population	0.069	0.143	0.220	0.309			
In work force	0.141	0.270	0.398	0.533			

Sources: Authors' estimates, based on background calculations and the following sources of work force estimates. The 1963 estimates are from Kingdom of Saudi Arabia, Ministry of Finance and National Economy, Directorate General of Statistics, *Hasr al Sukkan wal Mu'assasat, 1382 AH*, adjusted by the authors for expatriates not included. The 1970 estimates are from Kingdom of Saudi Arabia, Central Planning Organization, *[Second] Development Plan, 1395–1400 AH [1975–80]* (Riyadh: Ministry of Planning, 1975); and U.S. Department of Labor, Bureau of Labor Statistics, *Labor Law and Practice in the Kingdom of Saudi Arabia*, BLS Report no. 407 (Washington, D.C.: U.S. Government Printing Office, 1973). The 1975 estimate is a hybrid from J. Stace Birks and Clive A. Sinclair, *The Kingdom of Saudi Arabia and the Libyan Arab Jamahiriya: The Key Countries of Employment*, World Employment Program Research Working Paper, WEP 2-26/WP-39 (Geneva: ILO, May 1979), and the World Bank International Migration Project. The 1980 estimate is the authors', based on trends contained in the Saudi Ministry of Planning, *Third Development Plan 1400–1405 AH, 1980–1985 AH* (Riyadh, 1980).

areas. If this were in fact true, the nomadic population will have most likely become too insignificant both in absolute numbers and in proportion to the total or to the Saudi population to be of consequence as a source of labor supply during the 1980s.

The second source of ambiguity, even controversy, is the number of expatriates. Saudi Arabia is not unique in this regard. Estimates of expatriates have often been controversial and difficult to pin down with precision, even in some of the most industrially advanced countries, such as the United States.[8] The highly tentative nature of expatriate population estimates in Saudi Arabia should thus be appreciated.

Historically, some preliminary evidence of international labor inflows became available as the first stirrings of modernization began in Saudi Arabia in the 1950s. Traders from Yemen had long played an important role in the Saudi economy, which began to be consolidated in the 1950s and 1960s. Nationals of other Arab states played important roles in the education and health sectors as early as the 1950s. Non-Arabs, mainly Westerners, filled occupations in the oil sector. However, quantitative data on labor in general and labor imports in particular are not easy to come by before the 1960s. Even during the 1960s, labor data are imprecise for a number of reasons, including lack of record keeping, relatively open frontiers, especially to the South, imprecision regarding migrants who had originally entered for purposes of the *hajj* (pilgrimage), and lack of clear ethnic, linguistic, or cultural characteristics distinguishing some (Yemeni) migrants from some (Southern) Saudis.

Despite these reservations, some estimates of expatriate population are necessary—even if they are not definitive—in order to trace a trend. Table 3-1 shows estimates of expatriate population and their ratio to total population in recent years, based on rising crude participation rates. Thus, it is estimated that the total number of expatriates was only 250,000 in 1963, representing about 7 percent of the total population. It is suspected that most were concentrated in the Eastern (the oil sector) and the Western (trade, finance, and services) regions. Since the reasonably fast growth of the 1960s attracted expatriates in increasing numbers, it is estimated that their number had grown to about 680,000 by 1970. During the even faster growth of the 1970s, expatriates continued their substantial inflows into the country. By 1975, it is estimated that the expatriate population may have reached more than 1.3 million, even though official figures are reported at 0.79 million. Although the fast tempo of expatriate inflows continued through the rest of the decade, no detailed information regarding this total stock or the annual flows has yet been made available. The 1980 figure of more than 2 million expatriates (about 30 percent of the total population) cited in chapter 1 represents an informed guess.

The implications of these findings for labor supply in the past are also shown in table 3-1. From about 0.7 million in 1963, Saudi employment expanded steadily to slightly more than 1.0 million in 1975 and about 1.2 million in 1980. The implied rate of growth was slightly above that of Saudi population growth, about 3 percent a year. The picture for expatriate labor supply was far more dynamic. From about 115,000 workers in 1963 representing 14 percent of the total work force, the number expanded to 320,000 in 1970 (about 27 percent of the work force) and to 668,500 in 1975 (about 40 percent of the work force). The accelerated pace of growth of the economy and the limited supply of Saudi workers caused the volume of expatriate workers to expand further, to about 1.35 million in 1980 (about 53 percent of the work force).

The implications of these differential developments for labor supply in the future are self-evident. If the age structure of the Saudi population remains generally stable in the next two or three decades, the rate of growth of Saudi labor supply would be about the same as the rate of growth of Saudi population, in the 2.8–3.0 percent range. Expansion in the total demand for labor above 3.0 percent per year will therefore have to be met through labor imports. This is not to say that labor imports will occur only if there is a numeric imbalance between Saudi labor supply and total demand for labor. Labor imports will continue because of a mismatch between the *structures* of Saudi labor supply and total labor demand. For this reason, it would not be unusual to find some unemployed Saudis with little or no skills at some future time.

Age Distribution

On the basis of established demographic relationships, it is clear that a closed population—that is, one with no significant international migration and with relatively constant age-specific fertility and mortality schedules—will tend to attain a stable age distribution and a constant rate of increase. A decline in mortality will have a relatively small effect on the stable age distribution if fertility rates remain unchanged. Such a decline will result in a new stable population having a somewhat higher percentage under 15 years old, a younger average age, and a small increase in the percentage of persons over 60 years.

The observed development pattern of the Saudi population during the past forty years seems to be in harmony with these demographic relationships. Considering its social and economic characteristics and the fertility rates of nearby countries, the crude birth rate in Saudi Arabia is estimated to be about 45 per thousand population as of 1981.[9] There is no reason to assume that fertility rates deviated significantly from these high levels during the past half century. For example, although fertility information is scarce in Saudi Arabia, the average size of completed families (that is, the number of living children by the time the mother is 44 years old) is probably in excess of five children, based on published preliminary results of the 1974 census.[10] The result of such persistent high levels of fertility is an age distribution of a predominantly young population. The 1974 census shows the ratio of dependents to be more or less as expected: about half the population is less than 15 years old and 6 to 7 percent is 60 years of age and above. The remaining 45 percent of the population are in the range of 15–59 years, the most relevant group for labor supply. This distribution is about the same for Saudi males and females.

There are, however, some peculiarities in the reported sex distribution. The male-female ratio in the aggregate is about 106:100. Furthermore, within most age ranges there are numerically more males than females. This is contrary to the expected pattern of sex ratios in populations with similar demographic characteristics. The variations in the number of males and females across the age groups, especially above 40 years, were particularly unusual (figure 3-1). Under one year of age the sex ratio is a reasonable 105, but between one and four there were more females than males. Between ages 10 and 24 it went in the opposite direction, and also above age 40, especially at age 55–59 when there were 56 percent more males than females. Most likely, this pattern is a result of underenumeration of females. Similar findings have been observed in other Arab countries.[11]

It is the age structure of the expatriate population that stands out in figure 3-2. Compared with the distribution of the Saudi population (figure 3-3), the age distribution of the expatriate population is clearly skewed in favor of the economically active age groups. Nearly three-fourths of expatriate males and more than half of expatriate females are in the 15–59 year range. This sex-age distribution of expatriate labor is the expected selectivity profile of recent and temporary migrants. Since the only reason for expatriates to be in Saudi Arabia is work, the participation rate of expatriates not only was much higher than that for the Saudis, but it will continue to be so in the foreseeable future.

Spatial Distribution

Saudi Arabia is a geographically extended country with five distinct planning regions. During the past two decades those regions have developed at different rates and with variant focal points of economic activity. The East has emerged as a giant industrial region with oil at its

center. The West, traditionally the country's trading center, has strength-
ened its position. The Central region emerged as the hub of government
and financial activities. Only the South and North seem to have missed
the development thrust of the past two decades. According to the third
development plan (1980–85), however, policymakers are determined to
integrate these regions more fully into the mainstream of the dynamic
Saudi development process. The South, as the traditional agricultural
center, is to receive massive resources to modernize its agriculture. The
North is to host new industries and expand its infrastructure, as well as
modernize its agriculture.

Against this background a key question arises: Is there one labor
market in Saudi Arabia, or are there several regional markets? The
answer depends, crucially, on the extent to which specific regions have in
the past pursued, and can continue to pursue in the future, development

Figure 3-1. *Reported and Stable Sex Ratios of Saudi Nationals
by Age, 1974*

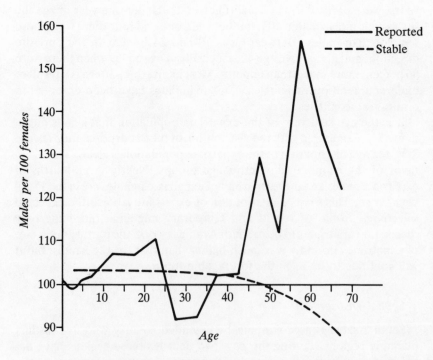

Source: United Nations Economic Commission for Western Asia (ECWA), *The Population Situation in the ECWA Region: Saudi Arabia* (Beirut: ECWA, 1979), fig. 11.3, p. 11.10.

without spillover effects on the other regions. Stronger regional linkages indicate a more integrated national labor market. By contrast, weak regional linkages are indicative of separate regional labor markets. In this respect, the historic pattern of Saudi development may be instructive. Precisely because of the great distances and difficulty of travel until recently between the various regions, the oil industry developed in the East during the 1940s, 1950s, and even the 1960s as an enclave economy with little or no relation to the other regions. In other words, the East did not exert much of a "pull effect" on the labor of the other regions. Furthermore, the development of the Eastern, Central, and Western regions during the 1970s seems to have produced little or no effects on the labor markets in the North and South. How much of that apparent labor market segmentation is because of a lack of interregional migration as opposed to the presence of expatriate workers, who filled new job open-

Figure 3-2. *Age-Sex Pyramid of the Non-National Population, 1974*

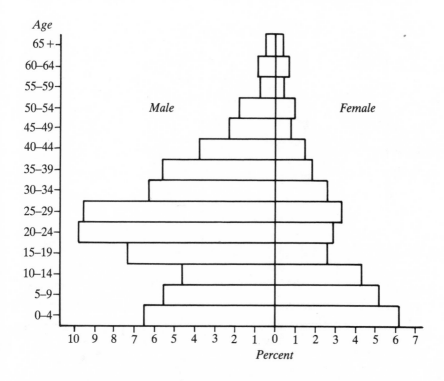

Source: ECWA, *The Population Situation*, fig. 11.2, p. 11.9.

ings before nationals had time to adjust, is an empirically testable hypothesis which will be examined in chapter 8.

If regional development in the past did not seem to have integrated the national labor market to a great extent, this does not mean it will be a self-perpetuating phenomenon. Saudi Arabia will remain a geographically extended country. However, transportation and communications between regions and with the outside world grew quite rapidly during the 1970s and are destined to grow even faster during the 1980s. Knowledge of regional opportunities and the increased ease of transporting capital and labor resources between regions are likely to increase the strength of regional linkages, and thus result in a nationally integrated labor market. Increased transportation and communications between regions, expanded awareness of regional business opportunities, and the easy transport of human and physical resources are but manifestations of mod-

Figure 3-3. *Age-Sex Pyramid of Saudi Nationals, 1974*

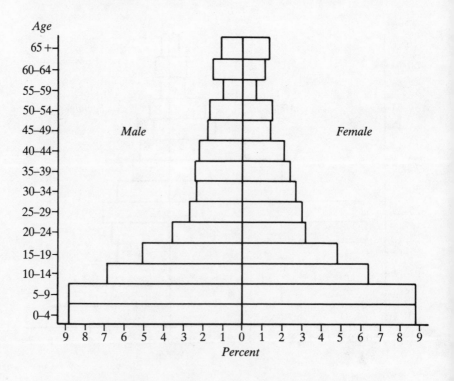

Source: ECWA, *The Population Situation*, fig. 11.1, p. 11.8.

ernization and urbanization, both of which seem to have been sweeping the Saudi economy.

To be sure, central government expenditures on regional development and regional resource balances, including labor resources, are intrinsically interdependent. Just as development expenditures during the 1970s created regional disparities, they can be aimed to reduce such disparities during the 1980s. For these reasons, this section focuses on the spatial distribution of the population.

As already indicated, no census data are available on the distribution of the population among the country's five regions. The data reported in table 3-2 represent the authors' best estimates for 1975, as obtained from a population projection exercise carried out in the World Bank in the late 1970s, subsequently modified by the authors.

As would be expected, the Western region has the largest population base. Although commercial and service activities have traditionally attracted Saudis, the boom of the 1970s generated such a demand for labor that it caused enormous expatriate inflows and by 1975 more than half the expatriates were living in the Western region. Expectedly also, the Northern region, with its low level of economic activity, has attracted the smallest number of both Saudis and expatriates. Between these two extremes fall the other three regions. The Central region has the second largest population base, both for Saudis and expatriates. The main activity there is government, finance, and related functions. The South comes next, where agriculture is the main activity of the population. Finally, the Eastern region contains the second smallest population, even though it is the center of the most important industry in the country. This is largely due to the highly capital-intensive nature of the oil industry.[12]

The relevance of this picture for the labor market is direct. Population clustering is highest in the West, medium in the Central and Southern regions, and lowest in the North and East. These clusters require variant levels of social services, including housing, and produce significant differentials in the incremental supply of labor. The largest source of labor

Table 3-2. *Regional Distribution of the Population*
(thousands; 1975 estimates)

Population	Eastern	Central	Northern	Western	Southern	Total
Saudi	537	1,140	528	1,494	1,041	4,740
Expatriate	151	266	43	688	192	1,340
Total	688	1,406	571	2,182	1,233	6,080

Source: Authors' estimates.

supply in the future will thus be the Western region, followed by the Central and Southern regions, then the Eastern and Northern regions.

A glimpse at the scarce information available on the population of selected cities over time shows the extent of urbanization between regions. Table 3-3 summarizes the available information. The cities which experienced the fastest growth of population were themselves the centers of the most characteristic economic activity for their respective regions. Thus, Riyadh experienced the fastest population growth precisely because the modernization of Saudi Arabia during the 1960s necessitated the increased role of both the central government and its services. Jeddah experienced a similar, though slightly less rapid, expansion because of the generally active role of trade, finance, and services in the development and growth of the Saudi economy during this period. Although Mecca and Medina experienced substantial urbanization during those same eleven years, more than doubling their population, such growth was still significantly less than that of Jeddah. In fact, although Jeddah's population was less than that of Mecca in 1963, it increased so rapidly that by 1974 it was about equal to the population of Mecca and Medina *combined*. The same logic applies in the Eastern region to the differential growth of the population of Hufuf and Dammam. These trends imply a tendency for the population to concentrate in limited areas. The overall density of the country is approximately 4 persons per square kilometer, rising to about 30 persons in the South, and dropping to almost none in the great deserts. According to the 1974 census, about 43 percent of the population was concentrated in two districts: 25 percent in the Mecca district and 18 percent in the Riyadh district.[13]

Table 3-3. *Population in Selected Cities*

Region	City	Population (thousands)		Index (1963 = 100)
		1963	*1974*	
Central	Riyadh	159	667	419
Western	Mecca	158	367	232
	Medina	72	198	275
	Jeddah	147	561	382
Eastern	Hufuf	51	101	198
	Dammam	35	128	366

Sources: Data for 1963 quoted in Zain Sebai, "The Health of the Bedouin Family in a Changing Arabia," Ph.D. dissertation, Johns Hopkins University, 1969, p. 6. Data for 1974 from Kingdom of Saudi Arabia, Central Department of Statistics, *Statistical Indicators* (Riyadh, 1978), p. 22.

Skill Formation

The discussion now moves from the quantitative considerations of labor supply to its qualitative aspects. Affecting the quality of labor supply are diverse factors such as literacy, education, nutrition, and health. The remainder of this chapter will focus on only two factors, literacy and education, which can be combined under the heading of skill formation. The other factors tend to be related in general to the average level of per capita income. In developing countries, a positive correlation exists between income per capita and the levels of nutrition and health. Saudi Arabia is no exception. The phenomenal growth of per capita income during the past two decades has undoubtedly contributed to significantly improved nutrition and health, although not uniformly in all regions, nor are these improvements reflected equally in the various measures of performance. For example, although life expectancy at birth increased from 38 years in 1960 to 53 years in 1979,[14] a remarkable achievement in such a short time, the infant mortality rate (that is, for those aged 0–1 years) was still about 118 per thousand live births in 1979 (compared with 38 for Kuwait, for example), and child death rates (ages 1–4 years) were 28 per thousand children compared with 2 for Kuwait.[15]

As for literacy, the 1974 census showed that 52 percent of all men and 79 percent of all women were illiterate. Grim as these figures appear, they are already a significant improvement over the situation prevailing two decades earlier. A good indicator is the age-specific data shown in table 3-4. Each age group is more literate than the next older one. This is generally true for both males and females, but more striking for males. In particular, for males entering the job market (age groups 15–19 and 20–24) the illiteracy rates are about half those of their fathers' generation (45 years and above). However, for each age group below 60 years of age female illiteracy rates are at least 20 percentage points above male rates. In view of the government's intensified efforts of the past few years to expand education and eradicate illiteracy, the age-specific data for the early 1980s should show a considerable improvement over that displayed in table 3-4.

This national picture is regionally disaggregated in table 3-5, which shows the literacy rates for males and females aged 10 years and above. The East has the lowest illiteracy rates for males and females. This is undoubtedly the result of two factors acting simultaneously. The first is the early concentration of the oil complex in the East, its subsequent spillover effects on related industries and services in the region, and the

Table 3-4. *Age-Specific Illiteracy Rates, 1974*
(percentage of the age groups)

Age group	Male	Female
10–14	35.3	59.2
15–19	39.3	66.3
20–24	43.3	76.0
25–29	47.3	83.6
30–34	50.0	88.4
35–39	55.7	90.9
40–44	62.8	93.8
45–49	67.1	93.6
50–54	73.7	95.2
55–59	76.0	94.2
60–64	83.3	95.8
65 +	85.2	96.0
Total	52.0	79.3

Source: Kingdom of Saudi Arabia, Central Department of Statistics, *Census of Population, 1394 AH [1974]* (Riyadh, n.d.), table 62.

Table 3-5. *Illiteracy Rates by Region*
(percent)

	East	Central	North	West	South
Male	42.5	44.9	66.2	49.5	64.9
Female	63.3	73.4	90.6	74.5	94.3

Source: Same as table 3-4.

correspondingly higher rates of educational attainment among the population. The second factor is probably urbanization. The government efforts to eradicate illiteracy are more easily targeted and undoubtedly more effective in urban centers than in remote rural villages. Thus, the Northern and Southern regions, both largely rural, have the highest incidence of male and female illiteracy. Although no significant differentials exist between North and South for either males or females, they do exist between these two regions and the remaining three. Another striking feature in regional illiteracy rates with potential implications for labor supply is the significant difference between male and female rates. Thus, in each region, female rates are *at least* 20 percentage points higher than male rates. Here, too, recent government efforts have made major strides in increasing female enrollments in literacy classes.

It is clear that the government has spared no effort to push educational development as much as it could. Government policy in human resource development is repeatedly articulated in all three development plans (see the appendix to this chapter). Even during the 1960s, prior to the introduction of central planning, nearly all measures indicate rapid growth of the various educational categories. Whatever the indicator—number of schools, classes, enrollments, graduates, or expenditures on education—all show a significantly upward trend, especially during the 1970s. Particular emphasis seems to have been placed on the development of specialized skills and high-level manpower. The results in terms of enrollments and graduates in those categories have been no less spectacular.

Table 3-6 shows the two expenditure items in national development plans with implications for skill formation: human resource development and social development. The first represents expenditures on education and vocational and technical training. The second includes expenditures on health care, family care, and child and youth care. Combined, they

Table 3-6. *Government Planned Allocations of Civilian Expenditures*
(millions of riyals)

Expenditure	First plan[a]		Second plan[b]		Third plan[c]	
	Amount	Percent	Amount	Percent	Amount	Percent
Economic resource development	2,693	8.5	92,135	21.9	261,800	33.4
Human resource development	7,378	23.2	80,124	19.1	129,600	16.6
Social development	1,921	6.0	33,213	7.9	61,200	7.8
Physical infra-structure	12,049	37.9	112,945	26.9	249,100	31.8
Administration	7,717	24.3	38,179	9.1	31,400	4.0
Emergency reserves, subsidies, external assistance	—	—	63,478	15.1	49,600	6.3
Total	31,758	100.0	420,074	100.0	782,700	100.0

— Not applicable.

a. From Kingdom of Saudi Arabia, Central Planning Organization *[First] Development Plan, 1390 AH* (Dammam: Al-Mutawa Press, 1970), table 2, p. 43, transformed from sector classification into functional classifications, in 1970 base prices.

b. From Kingdom of Saudi Arabia, Central Planning Organization, *[Second] Development Plan, 1395–1400 [1975–80]* (Riyadh: Ministry of Planning, 1975), table VIII-1, p. 600, in 1974–75 base prices.

c. From Kingdom of Saudi Arabia, Ministry of Planning, *Third Development Plan, 1400–1405 AH, 1980–1985 AD* (Riyadh, 1980), table 3-1, p. 88, in 1979–80 base prices.

represented 29, 27, and 24 percent, respectively, in the total allocations of the three plans. While the relative weight of skill-formation-related expenditures appears to have declined, they have nevertheless experienced phenomenal growth.

From an annual average of SR1.9 billion (1970 prices) during the first plan, government expenditures related to skill formation expanded to SR22.7 billion per year (1975 prices) during the second plan, and were planned at SR38.2 billion per year (1980 prices) during the third plan.[16] To compare these figures in real terms, only one base-year price must be used. The non-oil GDP deflator would be the appropriate yardstick. The Saudi Arabian Monetary Agency (SAMA) regularly publishes national accounts and related statistics, from which it is possible to construct the implicit deflator. Using 1970 as the base year (equals 100), 1975 appears to have a deflator index value of 222, and 1980 an index of 515.[17] Thus, compared with the first plan, annual government allocations for skill formation increased by about four times in the second plan, and by about three times in the third plan. Between the second and third plans, therefore, these allocations appear to have diminished in real terms, as did the total allocation for the entire development program. This reflects a reduction of capital spending and an increase in recurrent expenditures because of a shift in emphasis between the second and third development plans.

The outcome of this national commitment to skill formation can be measured in several ways. Table 3-7 shows the dramatic changes in three categories of general education. Starting with 1964–65 and ending with 1979–80, growth in the number of schools, classes, and enrolled students has been nothing less than phenomenal. In elementary education, each one of the three variables has at least quadrupled. The relative changes in the intermediate and secondary education categories have been even more dramatic. When these changes are considered incrementally to show the effects of the first and second plans, the rates of change are equally impressive.

A special indicator of skill formation, particularly its impact on social change, is the number of females enrolled in each one of those educational categories. The relative expansion of female enrollments in each case turned out to be significantly higher than the expansion in total enrollments. The result is the increased relative share of females in enrollments over time. For example, in elementary education, the ratio increased from 20 percent in 1964–65 to 38 percent in 1979–80. In intermediate education, the ratio increased from 6 to 33 percent, and in secondary education from 1 to 31 percent. Of particular interest is the accelerated pace of expanding female education across the educational

Table 3-7. *General Education Statistics*

Category	1964–65	1969–70	1974–75	1979–80
Elementary				
Schools	1,400	1,824	3,028	5,373
Classes	9,016	14,864	24,741	40,951
Total enrollment	224,468	397,153	634,498	862,260
Female enrollment	45,143	119,789	223,304	325,369
Intermediate				
Schools	126	352	647	1,377
Classes	630	2,034	4,624	9,368
Total enrollment	19,528	60,576	136,883	245,194
Female enrollment	1,154	5,305	38,544	80,087
Secondary				
Schools	23	64	182	456
Classes	156	500	1,366	3,521
Total enrollment	4,588	13,664	41,539	93,584
Female enrollment	52	1,487	10,206	28,957

Sources: For 1964–65, 1969–70, and 1974–75, Ministry of Education, Center for Statistical Data and Educational Documentation, *Educational Statistics in the Kingdom of Saudi Arabia* (Riyadh, 1969–70 and 1974–75); for 1979–80, Ministry of Finance and National Economy, Central Department of Statistics, *Statistical Year Book*, Seventeenth Issue (Riyadh, 1981), tables 2-2, 2-8, 2-12, 2-18.

categories: the ratio of female enrollment at any point in time is highest at the elementary level, followed by the intermediate, then the secondary.

For the specialized educational categories—teacher training, special, technical, adult, and university education—table 3-8 shows substantial growth in all variables and categories, though admittedly less explosive than that for general education. Each category has its own significance for skill formation in Saudi Arabia. Teacher training, by definition, has a multiplier effect. During the fifteen years under observation, the number of schools, classes, and total enrollments in this category more than doubled. Female enrollments showed an explosive growth, expanding from 8 percent of total enrollments in 1964–65 to 52 percent in 1979–80. The expansion in special education indicates the determination of the state not to leave behind either the handicapped or youths—male or female—with special problems. Adult education, in expanding as rapidly as it did, showed the interest of the state in raising the educational standards of its adult population and the receptivity of this segment of the population to such efforts. Both technical and university education have direct and immediate relation to the supply of high-level manpower and specialized skills. Developments in each warrant special attention.

Table 3-8. *Specialized Education Statistics*

Category	1964–65	1969–70	1974–75	1979–80
Teacher training				
Schools	47	49	76	107
Classes	294	358	494	829
Total enrollment	8,597	10,836	14,674	21,886
Female enrollment	710	6,492	3,840	11,434
Special education				
Schools	6	10	15	25
Classes	51	128	209	270
Total enrollment	652	1,248	1,784	1,920
Female enrollment	39	151	234	388
Technical education				
Schools	17	7	13	30
Classes	148	33	144	312
Enrollment	4,016	840	3,408	6,224
Adult education				
Schools	393	607	1,425	3,357
Classes	1,172	1,633	4,252	9,334
Enrollment	32,739	42,314	99,673	142,370
University education				
Colleges	11	18	22	n.a.
Total enrollment	2,997	6,942	19,093	47,733
Female enrollment	80	434	2,922	12,665
Graduates	398	808	1,885	n.a.

n.a. Not available.

Sources: Same as for table 3-7, plus *Statistical Year Book*, tables 2-13, 2-25, 2-26, 2-34, and 2-42.

Technical education seems to have been the only area where government efforts have fallen somewhat short of expectations. There was an actual decline during the 1960s in the number of schools, classes, and total enrollments for this type of education. It was not until the end of the second plan that enrollments exceeded their 1964–65 levels, and even then they were not up to the expectations of the second plan.

This change in total enrollment conceals the changes in the composition of technical education itself. The exclusively male technical education comprises three categories: agricultural, industrial, and commercial. Table 3-9 shows the dominance of industrial education in the mid-1960s: 56 percent, against 19 percent in agricultural and 25 percent in commercial. By 1969–70 the lowest enrollment in all technical education was reached, and commercial education nearly came to a halt. In the follow-

Table 3-9. *Technical Education: Male Students by Type and Level of Education*

Type and level of education	1965–66	1969–70	1974–75	1979–80
Agricultural				
Higher	—	—	—	—
Secondary	—	128	—	322
Intermediate	506	—	—	n.a.
Subtotal	506	128	—	322
Commercial				
Higher	—	—	—	264
Secondary	—	—	1,170	4,288
Intermediate	677	18	—	n.a.
Subtotal	677	18	1,170	4,552
Industrial				
Higher	—	—	105	n.a.
Secondary	130	692	2,133	1,213
Intermediate	1,400	2	—	n.a.
Subtotal	1,530	694	2,238	1,213
All technical				
Higher	—	—	105	264
Secondary	130	820	3,303	5,823
Intermediate	2,583	20	—	n.a.
Total	2,713	840	3,408	6,087

n.a. Not available.
— Nil or not applicable.
Sources: Same as for table 3-7; *Statistical Year Book*, table 2-34.

ing years agricultural education almost disappeared and both industrial and commercial expanded, particularly the latter. By 1979–80, agriculture represented about 5 percent of technical education, industry 20 percent, and commerce dominated with 75 percent. Apparently, the expansion in private sector activity proved to be sufficiently attractive for young Saudis to enroll in commercial and industrial education in increasing numbers during the 1970s. By 1980, however, the government was set to pursue an intensive revitalization of technical education that would also encompass agricultural education.

University education, the main source for high-level manpower and specialized skills, has shown impressive growth (see table 3-10). Enrollments have expanded over a fifteen-year period from less than 3,000 to more than 36,000. The number of graduates also expanded dramatically: from about 400 in 1964–65 to about 3,800 in 1978–79. Significantly, about

the same numbers of Saudis graduated in universities abroad, mostly in
the United Kingdom and the United States. Within Saudi Arabia itself,
arts and Islamic studies continued to dominate university enrollments
and graduates, but the expansion in the 1970s has been faster in areas
closely tied to the sectoral developments of the Saudi economy. Com-

Table 3-10. *University Enrollments and Graduates
by Major Academic Discipline*

Faculty	1964–65	1969–70	1974–75	1978–79
Arts				
Enrollments	773	1,651	4,478	7,588
Graduates	99	251	352	790
Commerce				
Enrollments	510	1,037	3,263	6,214
Graduates	40	62	177	519
Education				
Enrollments	190	578	3,168	5,492
Graduates	24	48	469	803
Science				
Enrollments	196	405	1,100	2,530
Graduates	24	27	106	165
Agriculture				
Enrollments	—	102	523	1,076
Graduates	—	22	61	119
Engineering				
Enrollments	198	847	2,177	4,972
Graduates	—	25	178	502
Pharmacy				
Enrollments	30	165	341	350
Graduates	11	10	39	46
Medicine				
Enrollments	—	35	276	1,674
Graduates	—	—	—	74
Islamic studies				
Enrollments	1,100	2,122	3,640	6,216
Graduates	200	363	503	761
All faculties				
Enrollments	2,997	6,942	18,996	36,122
Graduates	398	808	1,885	3,779

— Nil or negligible.
Source: Same as tables 3-7, 3-8, and 3-9.

merce, education, science, and engineering have been among the fastest growing branches of university education. The jobs and salaries which graduates of these disciplines have come to enjoy point to their continued growth in the 1980s to eclipse arts education. The allocations made in the third plan showed a continued commitment to the expansion of university education, especially in the areas of commerce, science, medicine, and engineering.

From the Second to the Third Development Plan

By 1980, the achievements of the second plan were manifest and the third plan was about to start. It was a good time to take stock.

As Saudi Arabia entered its second development decade, it could look back on a substantial record of achievement. During the previous five years, a high level of economic growth had been attained (an annual rate of about 13 percent for non-oil GDP) and a large proportion of the ambitious physical projects of the second plan had been implemented. The development of Saudi human resources was given a high priority. From 1975 to 1980 the physical facilities of the education and training system (ETS) expanded considerably. This capacity expansion, however, was not always matched by a commensurate increase in enrollments or graduates of the facilities in key areas such as primary education and teacher training, while other levels (intermediate and secondary) exceeded the second plan targets, thereby drawing students away from teacher training and technical and vocational schools and creating pressures for further expansion of academic university programs (see table 3-11).

The problem of underutilized facilities has been particularly marked in the case of technical and vocational education, where a variety of social and economic factors diverted students and trainees away from this type of education, in spite of the acute need for Saudi technicians and skilled workers. (The relation of institutional capacity to enrollment is presented in table 3-12.) Furthermore, apparently little has been done in pursuing qualitative improvements. The ETS was still inefficient, as indicated by the relatively high numbers of repeaters and dropouts, and was thus ill-suited to produce the type of manpower skills needed by the expanding Saudi economy. Various aspects of the ETS were improperly coordinated, with frequent duplication of effort, high costs, and lack of focus in the rapid and undirected growth of its component parts.

Against this background, the government launched the third plan programs with the following broad objectives:[18]

Table 3-11. *Targets and Achievements of the Second Five-year Plan in Enrollments and Schools*

Educational level	Enrollment (thousands)			Schools (number)		
	Target(T)	Achieved(A)	A/T (percent)	Target(T)	Achieved(A)	A/T (percent)
Elementary	638	514	80	2,089	3,940	124
Intermediate	125	155	124	644	936	145
Secondary	37	62	167	124	335	270
Teacher training	19	8	44	40	34	85

Table 3-12. *Institutional Capacity and Student Enrollment, 1978–79*

Type of training	Capacity(C)	Enrollment(E)	E/C (percent)
Vocational	6,200	2,500	40
Prevocational	700	300	43
Technical	17,000	6,500	38

- Making the ETS more responsive to the needs of the economy, by channeling its efforts toward improving the quantity and quality of the Saudi labor force and thereby reducing dependence on expatriates, particularly in occupations and sectors considered critical for national development. (This involves both in-service upgrading and training and preservice formal education and training programs.)
- Further expansion of the reach of the ETS, especially at the basic education level, to serve as large a percentage of the target populations as possible and achieve more equitable access to, and participation in, the ETS at the regional level.
- Improvement of the management of the system to control waste and inefficiency and to coordinate all concerned agencies (public and private) with a view to better training, allocation, and utilization of manpower. This should also include the development and implementation of programs and measures required for monitoring the impact and internal efficiency of the ETS, permitting in turn more effective planning, programming, and budgeting of its operation.
- Improvement of the quality of education and training programs generally.

To meet these broad objectives some of the initially planned expansion of physical plant was curtailed and attention was reoriented toward improving capacity utilization, consolidating management, and making qualitative improvements. This resulted in a realignment of planned investments to reduce capital investment somewhat and emphasize recurrent expenditures needed to achieve the qualitative goals. This is why planned total expenditures on skill formation appeared to decline (in real terms) between the second and third plans.

Remaining Problems and Issues

It is pertinent at this stage to review the problems and issues that faced the Saudi ETS in the early 1980s.

Physical Expansion

Although the ETS had expanded quite rapidly in the 1970s, this expansion was not always accompanied by a commensurate expansion in enrollments and graduates, especially in technical education. In addition, the facilities were frequently not ideally located in relation to the catchment areas.

Imbalanced Enrollments

The dispersed and changing (intraregional) population of Saudi Arabia has contributed to the uneven access to, and participation in, education. A major cause of imbalanced enrollments was, however, the poor locational planning of schools. The need to have schools near homes was particularly serious for girls at all levels of the general education program—as the government fully recognized. A further problem was the imbalance in enrollments within levels of the ETS. Particular problems at the turn of the decade included:

- General education: the lag in girls' enrollment behind those of boys at all levels; regional disparities in the percentage of the age group enrolled in basic education; and a continuing bias in secondary education toward the arts as opposed to science
- Technical and vocational education: declining enrollments as more students proceeded to secondary general education
- Teacher education: reduced enrollments in primary teaching colleges (partly because facilities had been converted into intermediate colleges); more intermediate teachers than elementary teachers; and generally low enrollments in all branches because of the low status of the profession
- Higher education: serious pressures on the administrative and instructional capacity of existing institutions from the rapid growth of enrollments; excessive enrollments in low-priority fields of study, largely as a continuation of the arts bias in secondary schools; and imbalances in the structure of enrollments because of excessive time required by students to complete their studies.

These problems are all surmountable, but they will clearly affect the pattern of new entrants into the labor force during the 1980s, given the long lead time required for ETS adjustments to be reflected in the ETS "output"—graduates and dropouts who leave to join the labor force.

Planning, Management, and Coordination

Undoubtedly, such a rapid pace of expansion as occurred during the years of the second plan must lead to some duplication and waste. The government rightly decided to focus on these problems during the third plan, initially by creating a national agency for manpower development, one of whose key responsibilities was to provide the necessary coordination and guidance to make the ETS both more efficient and more responsive to the requirements of the changing Saudi economy. It would thus integrate macro planning of manpower requirements with education and training (the supply function). It was also to remedy the lack of detailed information about skills most needed in the economy and their operational characteristics; to improve the irregular and inadequate access to basic statistical data caused by the prevailing distribution of ministerial responsibilities; and to provide appropriate lines of communication and feedback with supply agencies and with the clientele on the demand side. Such planning was to be complemented by better reporting and basic statistical analyses in the key responsible agencies, including tracer studies, which are essential for thoughtful and meaningful adjustments in the scope, content, and emphasis of education and training programs.

Even to improve reporting, however, will require some corollary improvements in technical staffing, organization, and management of the agencies involved. This will require both upgrading and systematic formal training of the personnel manning the ETS. Recognition of educational management as a key profession requires further emphasis—few universities have well-designed programs to address educational administration, and training abroad has remained a relatively ad hoc process.

Qualitative Improvement

There appears to be a general consensus that relatively few of the measures introduced by the government to improve the quality of education and training have met with success. Those that are generally considered successful, such as the provision of libraries to girls' schools, have not been fully evaluated and measures of their effectiveness are not known. Many promising programs, such as one to improve methods of teaching Arabic, science, and English (key to the medium-term development of the country), have been initiated but then have suffered from lack of follow-up. Other significant measures, such as the improvement of mathematics and science teaching (grades 1–12) and the design of new skill training programs (Ministry of Labor), have not been adequately analyzed in terms of rate of implementation, cost, and impact. An important task of the government in the third plan was therefore to set in motion institutionalized capabilities to launch educational innovations and special programs for improving the quality of the ETS, to monitor the performance of these programs, and to ensure follow-up, generalization, or redesign.

Training

Three types of training closely associated with the labor market—formal vocational education, upgrading, and on-the-job training—remain the most difficult challenges facing the government.

VOCATIONAL TRAINING. The Ministry of Labor's major attempt to provide further education and training for school graduates via its prevocational and vocational centers failed to attract sufficient entrants. The possible causes are many. Some undoubtedly stem from sociocultural preferences for nonmanual occupations. Other causes may be related to educational and administrative factors such as the low quality of the training programs, which still need revision; poorly trained teachers; inadequate linkages with the job market, which make it impossible to ensure jobs for graduates; and the low appeal of skilled jobs, in part because potential candidates lack knowledge about the private returns. In the third plan, the government planned to prepare and implement programs that would provide instruction more appropriate to the needs of individuals as well as of the economy.

UPGRADING. Given the rapidly changing employment opportunities of the Saudi work force, it appears that the second plan did not put enough emphasis on the upgrading and training of Saudis already in the work force. Such efforts as existed—the literacy campaign, for example—were rather unfocused and could have benefited from better planning and coordination. Despite a strong and beneficial labor law with regard to training and upgrading in the private sector, the results fell far short of expectations, and there was no systematic reporting on progress made in this area. Well-thought-out and systematic incentives have not been applied to upgrading (despite a general feeling that incentives have been tried and failed). Further, the corollary to the use of incentives—giving the target population better information and guidance about private costs and benefits—has not received sufficient attention (the data from our sample study, discussed later in this book, bears this out). Remedying all these areas was set as an objective of the government in the third plan.

ON-THE-JOB TRAINING. Although the evaluation of major industrial investments does take into account the on-the-job training of Saudis, it is not given sufficient attention despite the fact that the transfer of skills might be counted among the most significant benefits associated with many of these large projects. A commendable example is the work of the Saudi Arabian Basic Industries Corporation (SABIC), which is doing much to ensure that project-related training is well designed and appropriately financed. However, the country's overall requirements for highly skilled Saudis is certain to exceed the available supply for the next decade. The allocation of these key resources to competing agencies remains a critical question facing Saudi decisionmakers in the 1980s.

Entering the 1980s

To sum up: the development of the ETS since the mid-1960s, and the outstanding challenges facing the Saudi system in the 1980s, led to a concerted and thoughtful effort by the government in the third plan. The main emphasis is on making the ETS more responsive to the manpower needs of the economy; improving the management of the ETS, especially the higher education system; and improving the quality of education and training. Further expansion of physical facilities is to be much more deliberate than it has been, with emphasis on meeting established needs and on controlling design standards and implementation costs.

Findings of the Field Survey

It is now pertinent to review the findings of the field survey which are particularly relevant to labor supply, to contrast the survey parameters with the countrywide parameters outlined in this chapter, and to ascertain somewhat roughly the representativeness of the sample survey. Against the general background of skill formation in the country as a whole, it is instructive to present some of the findings of the field survey. Table 3-13 summarizes the educational attainment of the sample respondents (among Saudis only).

Notwithstanding the sample bias inherent in field surveys, the findings of table 3-13, when contrasted with those of the 1974 census, are nevertheless quite revealing. Closest to the census results would be the household sample taken in the summer of 1978: 38 percent of the respondents had no education; nearly all of them were male heads of households. In the 1974 census reported in table 3-4, the overall illiteracy rate for males

Table 3-13. *Distribution of Saudi Respondents by Educational Level*
(percent)

Educational level	Establishment sample		Household sample
	Public	Private	
None	19	20	38
Elementary	27	30	22
Secondary/intermediate	42	34	28
University/postgraduate	13	16	11
Total	100	100	100
Respondents (number)	1,050		867

was 52 percent, for the 10–14 year age group it was 35 percent, and for the 15–19 year age group, 39 percent. The passage of time undoubtedly contributed to the reduction in the illiteracy rates. The contrast of sample and census results supports the proposed hypothesis of an inverse relation between time and Saudi illiteracy.

Table 3-13 also shows that the largest percentage of illiterates is found among the household respondents. Not surprisingly, the ratio of illiterates in the establishment sample is about half that in the household sample, which indicates that some education is needed in order to be gainfully employed. Interestingly, 60 percent of the respondents in the household sample, but 50 percent or less in the establishment samples, had no secondary education. Correspondingly, significantly more respondents in the establishment samples (55 and 50 percent) than in the household sample (39 percent) attained at least a secondary education.

The vast majority of the Saudis in private establishments (91 percent) and in households (71 percent) did not have training of any kind. This reflects the difficulties the training programs have encountered, as discussed above. Those in the household sample who did have training were equally divided among managerial, clerical, technical, skilled, and other. Among Saudis in public establishments, the picture was different. A decidedly higher percentage reported past and current training: 56 percent of the total respondents, most of whom were in clerical occupations and the rest equally divided among managerial, technical, and other skills.

This account of country-wide developments and of the field survey indicates that the Saudis seem to have responded positively to the rapidly changing labor market. Their behavior reflects concerted efforts to improve the quantity and quality of available skills. Whether in the formal process of education or the less successful training programs, the indicators are all rising. Even the snapshot taken by the 1978 field survey appears to have caught a society in the midst of motion, notwithstanding its strongly traditional background and the short period during which much of the change took place.

Appendix. Human Resources and Development Plans

This discussion supplements the main text by examining in greater detail Saudi human resources and, particularly, measures taken to develop them in the three development plans. Government commitment to the development of human resources can be seen qualitatively and quantitatively in each of the three plan documents. For example, the first plan stated that the objectives of Saudi Arabia are "to maintain its religious and moral values and to raise the living standards and welfare of its people while providing for national security and maintaining economic and social stability." One of the three pillars to achieve these objectives is "developing human resources so that the several elements of society will be able to contribute more effectively to production and participate fully in the process of development." The document goes on to state that

> in the plan for manpower, an assessment is made of human resource requirements in the light of economic objectives adopted, likely supply-demand relationships, and the policies and measures to be taken to overcome any indicated imbalances. These are essential aspects in formulating the overall Plan, and the evaluations made show that substantial efforts will be needed for several years before a general state of self-sufficiency in manpower may be approached, and that continued participation of foreign labor will be essential.[19]

Thus, an early realization of the pivotal role of expatriate labor in Saudi Arabia is demonstrated, essentially to fill the gaps between the national supply of skills and those required by the development plan.

Similar sentiments were echoed in the Second Plan: "Among the fundamental values and principles which guide Saudi Arabia's balanced development is the development of human resources by education, training, and raising standards of health."[2] The elaboration of this objective, which moves from the technique orientation of the first plan to the policy orientation of the second, is worth reproducing:

> All the people of Saudi Arabia will have access to educational and training facilities at all levels, and health services will be provided throughout the Kingdom.

Education and training—free of charge at all levels—will continue to expand and improve in quality, with the aim not only of eradicating illiteracy and promoting learning, but also to teach new skills, to stimulate research and the use of production and distribution techniques, and to inculcate the spirit of honest hard work.

To achieve the full potential of the Kingdom's human resources requires the creation of a healthy social and physical environment combined with an adequate free medical service throughout the country in fully-equipped hospitals, dispensaries, and health centers.

An economic climate will be created that enables the individual to find gainful employment in accordance with his capabilities, to depend on himself in earning his living, and to contribute to the development of his country.[21]

Having gone through the unusual years of the 1970s, which amply demonstrated the central role of human resources in the development of Saudi Arabia, the government articulated its policies in the third plan document in a much more specific form. Only an excerpt from that document can convey the sense of the government's purpose in developing human resources and the degree of specificity in formulating the necessary policies:

Manpower Development. Manpower development has the highest national priority, since the effective utilization of available manpower is the key element in the whole strategy for the Third Plan. There are four particular objectives for manpower development: to increase the total numbers of available manpower; to increase the productivity of manpower in all sectors; to deploy manpower to those sectors with the greatest potential for growth and highest productivity levels; to reduce dependence on foreign manpower.

These objectives will be achieved through a comprehensive set of policies which, in combination, will directly or indirectly implement far-reaching changes in the allocation and development of manpower. These policies cover educational, training, research and administrative measures. The strategy for manpower development, and its implementation throughout the economy and society, will be administered through measures to be recommended by the Inter-Ministerial Committee for Manpower, which was established in the last year of the Second Plan, or by any new modified agency recommended by this Committee.

Certain particular new policies will be introduced during the Third Plan, as follows:

(1) *Education.* As primary education is indispensable, sufficient numbers of schools and teachers will be provided for all boys and girls of primary school age. Beyond the intermediate level, there will be streaming of students so that appropriate proportions of the total student body continue in formal education or are guided towards specialized technical training institutes, in accordance with the national needs for various types of skilled manpower. Grants for university students will be limited to students who maintain a good level of proficiency, and who are specializing in subjects which are considered to require extra incentives. The curricula of primary, intermediate, secondary and university level education will be reviewed in accordance with the principles of the Sharia and the changing needs of society and of the economy.

(2) *Training.* The private sector will be encouraged to expand training programs, and the award of significant government loans to private industry will be conditional on the recipient including a full training scheme for Saudis in the project. Training schemes will be monitored to ensure that they are in keeping with the real needs of the Kingdom, and on-the-job training will be emphasized. In order to assist the recruitment of Saudis in training schemes, the Government will reappraise the range and system of incentives to encourage citizens to train for, and seek employment in, technical and skilled jobs.

(3) *Redeployment of Manpower.* Surplus manpower currently employed in remote areas and sectors with limited economic potential will be encouraged to move to areas and sectors with opportunities for employment in productive activities. In the Government, all fit and able younger men will be progressively transferred out of unskilled non-cadre positions and into training schemes or productive activities.

(4) *Manpower Planning and Management.* Research will be expanded to provide the basic statistics and general information concerning the present distribution and future development of manpower. This will be done in close cooperation between the universities and the government ministries concerned. The Government itself will undertake a comprehensive survey of the distribution of its own manpower resources in terms of the priorities and the needs of the various agencies and the private sector. It will also inform a committee of the Council of Ministers to identify the basis and areas of work for women, which do not conflict with the principles of Islam. The Government will also use the expertise and manpower of the universities and the Armed Forces to participate in implementing and supervising important development projects.[22]

This long-term commitment to human resource development in general and to skill formation in particular can also be seen in the budgetary allocations in all three plans, as noted in the text of chapter 3. It can be understood in the context of a prevalent long-term vision of Saudi society in the twenty-first century: a dynamic, *productive* society, with a diversified economic base, in which all citizens will be guaranteed basic needs and welfare and all able citizens will be well-educated, productive participants in the country's ongoing development. There is no intention of creating a society of *rentiers* with continued dependence on foreign labor. The presence of foreign labor is seen primarily as a necessary short-term and intermediate-term measure to expedite the desired social and economic transformation. In the longer term, Saudi policymakers see foreign labor playing a small and declining role in the country's socioeconomic structure. A real challenge for Saudi society will be its ability to maintain some continuity in its cultural values and retain its Islamic identity throughout this period of rapid social and economic modernization.

Accordingly, the development of Saudi human resources stands at the heart of the development process. Healthy, well-nourished, well-educated, productive individuals, who retain their sense of identity through cultural continuity, will manage their own affairs in their own way. To achieve this, the national ETS plays a central role, in coordination with health, nutrition, and other related programs, as does a flexible institutional structure that can adapt to the exigencies of rapid change and modernization.

From the preceding vision of Saudi society it is evident that education is seen as serving two functions. The first is to provide a fundamental service to which every citizen has access as a matter of right (part of this service will preserve the self-identity of youths by giving a sense of cultural continuity and by transmitting Islamic values to succeeding generations of Saudis). The second function is to provide training to equip future participants in the labor force with appropriate skills for productive employment. The ETS must therefore strive to expand its coverage so that all citizens have access to basic education and to provide appropriate training in response to the needs of the economy.

Notes

1. United Nations Economic Commission for Western Asia (ECWA), *The Population Situation in the ECWA Region: Saudi Arabia* (Beirut: ECWA, 1979). This source contains a detailed bibliography of demographic studies relating to Saudi Arabia.

2. Although official censuses, demographic surveys, and regional surveys by international consulting firms have been conducted intermittently since 1962, observers of the Saudi economy continue to disagree about several features of the population: the total size, the distribution between Saudis and expatriates, the number of nomads, and even the age structure and its division into males and females. Unless otherwise noted, figures provided in this chapter are the authors' best estimates, in view of the inconsistencies in available data.

3. R. McGregor, "Saudi Arabia: Population and the Making of a Modern State," in John I. Clarke and W. B. Fisher, eds., *Population of the Middle East and North Africa* (London: University of London Press, 1972), pp. 220–41.

4. ECWA, *The Population Situation*, pp. 11–14.

5. From Kingdom of Saudi Arabia, Central Department of Statistics, *Census of Population, Buildings and Establishments 1962/63* and the *Establishments Survey, 1963* (Riyadh, 1963), total employment in 1963 was estimated at 723,000, of which 662,000 were estimated to be Saudi nationals. A crude participation rate of 20 percent, seemingly consistent with the sociocultural characteristics of neighboring countries, would put the estimate of Saudi population in 1963 at 3.31 million. See Birks and Sinclair, *The Kingdom of Saudi Arabia*.

6. Birks and Sinclair, *The Kingdom of Saudi Arabia*, p. 9.

7. See A. R. Al-Madani and M. Al-Fayez, as reported in R. El Mallakh, *Saudi Arabia Rush to Development* (Baltimore, Md.: Johns Hopkins University Press, 1982), table 1.1, p. 21.

8. Considerable variation is found in the estimates of the Mexican population in the United States, even among different U.S. government agencies. For a detailed discussion of this controversy and the method employed by various researchers to arrive at their estimates, refer to Charles B. Keely, "Illegal Migration," *Scientific American*, vol. 240, no. 3 (March 1982), p. 43, which lists nine separate estimates of illegal residents made in the 1970s, and to Shahid Javed Burki, ed., *International Migration* (Washington, D.C.: The World Bank, forthcoming).

9. The World Bank, *World Development Report 1983* (New York: Oxford University Press, 1983), table 20, pp. 186–87.

10. Quoted in ECWA, *The Population Situation*, pp. 11.7–11.11.

11. ECWA, *The Population Situation*, p. 11.7.

12. ARAMCO, the largest single producer of oil in the world outside the U.S.S.R., employs approximately 14,000 persons. In the petrochemical plants being developed in Jubail (Eastern province) investments of $1.5 million to $2.0 million per job are not uncommon. These figures, however, do not include secondary employment effects of these major economic activities.

13. ECWA, *The Population Situation*, pp. 11.4–11.5.

14. It had reached 55 years by 1981 (*World Development Report 1983*, table 23, p. 193).

15. The corresponding Saudi data for 1960 were an infant mortality rate of 185 per thousand live births and a child death rate of 48 per thousand children, again showing a dramatic decrease. By 1981, figures had fallen still further, to 111 and 17 per thousand, respectively (*World Development Report 1983*, table 23, p. 193).

16. The Saudi riyal (SR) in 1983 was equal to about US$0.30. The relation between the riyal and the dollar was remarkably stable during 1973–83. "Billion" is used throughout in the sense of thousand million.

17. Kingdom of Saudi Arabia, Saudi Arabian Monetary Agency, Research and Statistics Department *Annual Report, 1400* (Riyadh, December 1980), table 9, p. 9.

18. For a fuller discussion of the objectives of human resource development in Saudi Arabia see the appendix to this chapter.

19. Kingdom of Saudi Arabia, Central Planning Organization, *[First] Development Plan, 1390 AH [1970–75]* (Dammam: Al-Mutawa Press, 1970), p. 23.

20. Kingdom of Saudi Arabia, Central Planning Organization, *[Second] Development Plan, 1395–1400 AH [1975–80]* (Riyadh: Ministry of Planning, 1975), p. 1.

21. Ibid., p. 2.

22. Kingdom of Saudi Arabia, Ministry of Planning, *Third Development Plan, 1400–1405 AH, 1980–1985 AD* (Riyadh, 1980), pp. 83–84.

4. Labor Demand and Its Dynamics

ANALYSIS OF THE LABOR MARKET is, by definition, incomplete without analysis of labor demand and its dynamics. It is true that the thrust of this book is on labor supply, and more specifically the Saudi component of labor supply. It is equally true, however, that labor demand and supply are so intimately linked that what is observed in the marketplace is not labor supply separate from labor demand, but the outcome of supply and demand combined: employment, wages, and the institutions governing the behavior of workers and employers. To be sure, the labor market does not necessarily produce equilibrium between labor supply and demand. There are always residuals of the market forces: unemployed workers seeking jobs and job vacancies continuing unfilled. Despite the common ground of the marketplace which binds labor supply and demand, conceptual and empirical tools of analysis separate the two. The focus of this chapter will be the forces underlying the demand for labor in Saudi Arabia.

The analysis of demand will be carried out at two closely linked levels: macro and sectoral. The macro level will by necessity be limited to the size of aggregate labor demand over time. The sectoral level will capture changes in the structure of demand for labor over time. In both cases, activity level—that is, output of the non-oil sectors—is postulated as the main determinant of the demand for labor.

Aggregate Labor Demand

Labor demand at the macro level is intimately linked to the growth of the Saudi economy over time. A review of nearly three decades of growth performance shows the central role which oil revenues have played in the economy and, by implication, in labor demand.

During the 1950s, the rate of growth of gross domestic product (GDP) in real terms is estimated to have been a little below 6 percent a year, almost identical to the rate of growth of oil production. During the 1960s, growth of GDP increased to 8 percent a year in association with the acceleration of oil production at 11.5 percent a year. During the 1970s, however, it became necessary to distinguish between oil GDP and non-oil GDP, and between the first half and the second half of the decade. Compared with the 1960s, growth of both non-oil GDP and oil production accelerated during 1970–75: to 10.4 percent and 13.2 percent a year, respectively. During 1975–80, however, while growth of non-oil GDP accelerated further to 13.1 percent, growth of oil production, thanks to the unprecedented increases in oil prices, decelerated significantly to about 7 percent a year.[1]

It has already been argued elsewhere that the era of capital-constrained development ended and a new era of labor-constrained development began early in the 1970s.[2] For this reason, 1970 serves as a point of departure in reviewing past developments in the aggregate demand for labor.

In assessing the relationship of accelerated growth of the Saudi economy and the aggregate labor demand, the so-called production function will be the guiding principle of the analysis. The production function is a stable relationship between output and changes in labor and capital inputs. Problems of estimating production functions in highly industrialized societies are well known, despite the availability of fine and reliable data on labor inputs. In Saudi Arabia such data are available only sporadically. No attempt can therefore be made to construct a production function for the Saudi economy. However, the logic underlying the production function may be employed to develop a sort of gross measure of the relation between output and labor. To be sure, such a labor-output coefficient must by definition contain a statistical bias resulting from the inevitable exclusion of capital inputs for the reasons just stated.

Furthermore, while the standard notion of the production function considers output as a function of labor, what is used here is another version—one which states labor "requirements" for a given level of output. Accordingly, the emphasis will be on the change in labor input which is necessary to produce specific changes in output. The labor elasticity of output (q) may thus be defined as the relative change in labor input (dL/L) corresponding to a given relative change in (non-oil) output (dV/V). Specifically, $q = (dL/L)/(dV/V)$.

Only discontinuous data are available on labor and output for the same periods. The labor elasticity of output thus defined would then be estimated from fragmentary information, and for time intervals only (that is, no annual observations). The published estimates on employment in Saudi Arabia come from voluminous studies done by various organizations and researchers on specific years and are therefore not easily reconcilable. The best estimates the present authors were able to put together from such published sources are as follows: in 1963 total employment was about 815,000; in 1970 it was 1,187,300; in 1975 it was 1,679,200; and in 1980 it is estimated at 2,525,000 (see table 3-1 above). These estimates produce annual growth rates of employment for the time intervals indicated as 5.5 percent, 7.2 percent, and 8.5 percent, respectively. Combining these estimates with growth of non-oil GDP for the same time intervals computes the labor elasticity of output (q) shown in table 4-1.

This table reveals that the accelerated growth of non-oil GDP was indeed closely associated with accelerated growth in employment. Although the data reported here are of a somewhat tentative nature, especially those of the 1960s, they give what appear to be plausible results. They suggest that during a seventeen-year period of observations, decomposed into three subperiods, the labor elasticity of output was generally stable at about 0.7. This means that, on average, an increase of one percentage point in the growth of the (non-oil) economy was generally associated with a 0.7 percent expansion in employment. To be sure, there was a slight decline in q during the second half of the 1970s, but that it remained stable throughout the period at around 0.7 is a remarkable, or simply fortunate, finding. Its implications for policy discussion and for planning the future of the kingdom are self-evident.[3]

The relative stability in the labor elasticity of output over a reasonably long period masks another remarkable development of the Saudi economy. Computing the average labor productivity in terms of the value added in the non-oil sectors per employed person per year, one finds a

Table 4-1. *Estimation of the Labor Elasticity of Output (q)*

Period	Growth of non-oil GDP (dV/V) (percent)	Growth of employment (dL/L) (percent)	$q = (dL/L)/(dV/V)$
1963–70	8.1	5.5	0.68
1970–75	10.4	7.2	0.69
1975–80	13.1	8.5	0.65

Sources: Growth of non-oil GDP from several sources, including the following: For 1963–70 and 1970–75, from Sherbiny and Serageldin, "Expatriate Labor and Economic Growth," table III. For 1975–80, from International Monetary Fund, *International Financial Statistics* (Washington, D.C., annual); Saudi Arabian Monetary Agency (SAMA), *Annual Report* (Riyadh); and *Statistical Summary* (Riyadh, annual). Growth of employment from table 3-1 above.

significant acceleration in the growth of average productivity over the same period. Thus, while the growth of average productivity was 2.4 percent a year during 1963–70, it accelerated to 3.0 percent a year during 1970–75, and to 4.2 percent a year during 1975–80. Undoubtedly, such acceleration in the growth of productivity was, at least in part, the result of the massive increases in investment over time. Gross domestic investment per employed person in real terms is estimated by the authors to have grown at about 6 percent a year in the 1960s and at about 18 percent a year during 1970–75; it decelerated somewhat during 1975–80 to about 16 percent a year. Capital per unit of labor in the Saudi economy increased during the 1970s beyond what any observers could have fantasized on the eve of the great oil price explosion of 1973.

The acceleration of productivity growth, which appears to have been closely associated with the acceleration in the growth of non-oil GDP, is a significant finding. It is compatible with the so-called Verdoorn law, which was developed from a reliable data base in a number of industrially advanced countries. Simply stated, Verdoorn formulated an empirically based hypothesis which suggests a significant positive association between rates of economic growth and rates of average productivity growth.[4]

The accelerated growth in the demand for labor could not possibly have been met from the Saudi supply of labor alone, which was increasing at a stable rate of about 3 percent a year. The gap between total demand for labor and domestic supply of labor, itself growing over time, had to be bridged by expatriate labor. Estimates of expatriate labor in Saudi Arabia, made in several studies and reports by various organizations and researchers are, as already indicated in chapter 3, problematic and difficult to reconcile over time. From the same sources cited in estimating total employment, the best estimates the present authors were able to put together appear in table 4-2. The figures show an unusually high growth

Table 4-2. *Estimates of Saudi and Expatriate Employment, 1963–80*
(thousands of persons)

Employment	1963	1970	1975	1980
Saudi	700.0	867.3	1,010.7	1,178.0
Expatriate	115.0	320.0	668.5	1,347.0
Total	815.0	1,187.3	1,679.2	2,525.0
Expatriates (percentage of total)	14.1	27.0	39.8	53.3

Source: Table 3-1, above.

of expatriate labor, ranging from 15.7 percent during 1963–70, to 15.9 percent during 1970–75, to 15.0 percent during 1975–80. These rates are about five times the rates of growth of Saudi labor. These high growth differentials kept pushing the expatriate labor ratio to ever higher levels, doubling from 14 percent in 1963 to 27 percent in 1970, and doubling again in 1980 to more than 53 percent.

Sectoral Labor Demand

The accelerated growth of the non-oil economy in association with that of both labor demand and overall labor productivity gives only part of the labor demand picture. The other part is the resultant changes in the structure of the non-oil GDP and the corresponding changes both in the structure of labor demand and in the growth of sectoral productivity. For the purposes of this chapter, sectoral detail will be presented according to the three-way classification of primary, secondary, and tertiary sectors. The primary sector comprises agriculture and (non-oil) mining. The secondary sector covers manufacturing (oil and non-oil), utilities, transport, and construction. The tertiary sector combines all the rest, including trade, finance, and public and social services.

Studies of economic growth, whether in developed or developing countries, have established that significant changes in the structure of output and employment usually accompany such growth. Furthermore, these changes have predictable trends.[5] Thus, as the economy grows, the relative share of the primary sector in total employment declines, and those of the secondary and the tertiary sectors expand. How closely these changes are associated with growth is, of course, a matter which varies among countries and even for the same country over time.

The Saudi economy is no exception. An attempt is made here to trace the structures of non-oil GDP and employment since 1963 to show the extent to which changes in those structures accompanied the accelerated growth of the economy. Table 4-3 shows that those structures have shifted significantly during less than two decades. Indeed, it appears that some of those shifts would have taken generations in other countries. These rapid shifts may therefore be explained by the continued acceleration of growth of the non-oil economy. In no other country has the relative share of the primary sector declined from 16 percent to 6 percent of GDP (non-oil) and from 58 percent to 21 percent of total employment (non-oil) in less than twenty years. Such developments indicate that the demand for labor in the secondary and tertiary sectors accelerated to the point of literally pulling out some labor from the primary sector. Not only

Table 4-3. *Structure of Employment and Non-oil GDP, 1963–80*

	1963	1970	1975	1980
Employment				
Thousands of persons	815.0	1,187.3	1,679.2	2,525.0
Percentage distribution				
Primary	58.3	44.6	34.5	21.4
Secondary	10.9	17.0	24.0	29.0
Tertiary	30.7	38.4	41.5	49.6
Non-oil GDP				
Millions of riyals	5,663.0	9,047.0	14,895.0	27,456.0
Percentage distribution				
Primary	16.0	11.4	8.7	6.4
Secondary	34.7	45.6	50.0	44.9
Tertiary	50.5	43.0	41.3	48.7

Note: The primary sector includes agriculture and non-oil mining; the secondary sector includes oil and non-oil manufacturing, utilities, transport and storage, and construction; and the tertiary sector includes all the rest such as trade, finance, and social and government services.

Sources: Authors' estimates, based on table 3-1 for employment, and on table 4-1 for non-oil GDP, in constant 1969–70 prices.

did the relative share of the primary sector in total employment fall, but the absolute numbers employed in that sector also declined, especially during 1975–80.

Also noteworthy is the rapid expansion in the relative employment shares of the secondary and tertiary sectors. These shifts complement the shifts observed in the share of the primary sector. Together, the figures reported in table 4-3 are indicative of the diversification which has been sweeping Saudi society.

Accompanying such changes in the structure of employment were equally important and significant changes in the occupational structure of the labor force. Let occupations be tentatively classified by skill level into high, medium, and low. The high-skill category refers to professionals, managers, and administrators. The medium-skill category refers to clerical, sales, and service workers. The low-skill category refers to farmers, fishermen, craftsmen, and laborers. Comparative data for these categories are available only for 1974 and 1978. Such a short period could hardly be expected to show change in the occupational structure of the labor force, particularly its Saudi component. The true surprise, however, is that significant shifts do take place, and the changes are compatible with the change in the structure of employment.

For example, the skill profile of the Saudis for 1974 was 12 percent for high skills, 43 percent for medium skills, and 45 percent for low skills. The 1978 profile shows substantial improvement in skill distribution, undoubtedly the result of concerted efforts at skill formation, and possibly some realignment in the entry requirements for certain occupations. The partial data available seem to indicate that the respective ratios have become 23 percent, 54 percent, and 23 percent for the stated skill levels. Thus, the shares of high- and medium-skill categories increased at the expense of the low-skill categories. The picture is more specifically detailed in chapter 5 (see table 5-3).

Contrasting the rates of growth for sectoral employment and output, it is possible to compute the sectoral labor elasticity of output for three subperiods: 1963–70, 1970–75, and 1975–80. Table 4-4 shows such elasticity estimates. The figures demonstrate that even though the elasticity estimate at the aggregate level of the (non-oil) economy was generally stable, the sectoral elasticity estimates, particularly for the primary and tertiary sectors, were anything but stable. In both the primary and tertiary sectors, elasticity estimates were declining significantly over time. This is an indication of improved productivity performance. The elasticity estimate for the primary sector during 1975–80 was negative, indicating that growth in output was accomplished with reductions in the sector's work force. In the secondary sector, however, elasticity estimates not only were above unity, but seem to have been increasing as well. Such figures indicate two unhappy developments: a given percentage increase in secondary sector output was associated, on average, with a more than proportional increase in employment, and as a result, average labor productivity was declining.

Of particular interest is to compare the elasticities for 1975–80 estimated from the actual performance of the economy with those underlying the second development plan. For the primary sector, the elasticity estimate based on actual observations was -0.22. Remarkably, the plan envisioned an elasticity of -0.25. It appears that the actual labor-output relation for this sector was in line with what was planned: to achieve

Table 4-4. *Sectoral Labor Elasticity of Output*

Sector	1963–70	1970–75	1975–80
Primary	0.89	0.38	-0.22
Secondary	1.11	1.18	1.20
Tertiary	2.00	0.93	0.74
Total non-oil economy	0.68	0.69	0.65

Source: Authors' estimates, based on data and background calculations for table 4-3.

output growth targets and reduce the work force in the sector. For the secondary sector, where elasticity based on actual observations was 1.20, that implied in second plan calculations was a close 1.13. Especially noteworthy is that employment was planned to expand faster than output, a rather peculiar prospect for the secondary sector. Such planned rates may be justified, however, when new projects have considerable gestation lags between employment expansion and output expansion— quite a likely possibility for the Saudi economy. The only significant discrepancy in sectoral elasticity estimates between actual observations and planning calculations is for the tertiary sector. Whereas the planned elasticity was slightly above 1.0, actual observations produced an estimate of 0.74, meaning that it was possible to attain output targets with relatively less employment expansion than had been planned.[6]

The preceding analysis of labor demand will by definition be lacking if it is limited only to the labor-output elasticity method. Such analysis should ideally be complemented by the so-called productivity growth method. The two methods complement each other in that the strength of one makes up for the deficiencies of the other, whether at the aggregate or the sectoral level. The elasticity method computes labor requirements directly from output growth figures. However, the implied productivity growth varies directly with output growth rates. For given elasticity estimates, higher output growth rates imply higher productivity growth rates, and vice versa. The elasticity method thus does not conflict with the Verdoorn law, especially in an ex ante sense. As such, it is a handy tool at the disposal of the manpower planner. The productivity growth method, by contrast, computes manpower requirements by combining output growth with productivity growth. This is an especially useful tool in situations where a planner has a good feel from past experience for the likely output growth rates and productivity growth performance, at the aggregate or sectoral levels. One can easily assess whether the economy as a whole or a specific sector is accelerating or decelerating its growth performance. It is not possible to do so when using the elasticity method.

Table 4-5 shows sectoral growth rates of employment, GDP, and productivity. Here, a much richer picture of sectoral labor demand over time emerges. One can compare the growth of sectoral labor demand over time for a given sector or for a given period across sectors. The demand for labor expanded fastest in the secondary sector, followed at some distance, except for 1975–80, by the tertiary sector. The demand for labor expanded slowest in the primary sector, and declined in absolute terms during 1975–80. Such development is a demonstration of the serious efforts to diversify the production base of the Saudi economy. Another demonstration of such efforts is the markedly higher rates of output

Table 4-5. *Average Annual Rates of Growth of Employment, GDP, and Productivity, 1963–80*
(percent)

Sector	1963–70	1970–75	1975–80
Primary			
Employment	1.6	1.8	−1.4
GDP	1.8	4.7	6.3
Productivity	0.3	2.8	7.7
Secondary			
Employment	12.4	14.8	12.7
GDP	11.2	12.6	10.6
Productivity	−1.0	−2.0	−1.8
Tertiary			
Employment	9.0	8.9	12.4
GDP	4.5	9.6	16.8
Productivity	−4.1	0.7	3.9
Total			
Employment	5.5	7.2	8.5
GDP	8.1	10.5	13.0
Productivity	2.4	3.1	4.2

Source: Authors' estimates, based on data and background calculations for table 4-3.

growth in the secondary and tertiary sectors, by comparison with those in the primary sector.

When rates of growth of sectoral employment and output are combined, sectoral productivity growth performance can thus be ascertained. The sector which recorded the most spectacular growth in productivity, by far, has been the primary sector. Accelerated growth in primary sector productivity was the sine qua non which enabled the substantial shifts of Saudis from rural to urban areas. Indeed, thanks to such high rates of productivity growth, employment in the primary sector actually declined in absolute terms by 1980, as already indicated.

The secondary sector, by contrast, experienced some of the most dynamic changes in output and employment, yet the least satisfactory change in productivity. Although output expanded at a minimum of nearly 11 percent a year, employment expanded at no less than 12 percent a year. Precisely because employment expanded faster than output, the productivity performance has been along a declining trend. The average productivity in 1980 was *below* its 1963 level by about 23 percent.

The tertiary sector experienced generally accelerated growth in employment, and a faster acceleration in growth of output. Even though productivity growth accelerated significantly during the 1970s, it could not compensate for the initial decline during the 1960s. The average productivity in 1980 was *below* its 1963 level by about 7 percent.

Finally, the data contained in table 4-5 allow for the empirical testing of the Verdoorn law in the Saudi context. The close association between growth of sectoral output and growth of sectoral productivity was found to hold for the primary sector, the tertiary sector, and for the economy at large; it did not hold for the secondary sector. Ironically, the secondary sector usually lends itself most readily to supporting the Verdoorn law. The conclusion which emerges at this juncture is that, notwithstanding some of the highest growth of output, the demand for labor in the secondary sector appears to have expanded faster than was justified by sensible economic calculations. The implications of this conclusion for policymaking in the kingdom are self-evident.

Notes

1. Estimates of growth of GDP and oil production for the 1950s and 1960s are obtained from Naiem A. Sherbiny and Ismail Serageldin, "Expatriate Labor and Economic Growth: Saudi Demand for Egyptian Labor," in *Rich and Poor States in the Middle East: Egypt and the New Arab Order*, Malcom H. Kerr and El Sayed Yassin, eds., Westview Special Studies on the Middle East (Boulder, Colo.: Westview Press; Cairo, Egypt: American University in Cairo Press, 1982), pp. 225–57.

2. Naiem A. Sherbiny, "Sectoral Employment Projections with Minimum Data: The Case of Saudi Arabia," in Naiem A. Sherbiny, ed., *Manpower Planning in the Oil Countries*, Supplement 1 to *Research in Human Capital and Development: A Research Annual* (Greenwich, Conn.: JAI Press, 1981), pp. 173–206; and Sherbiny and Serageldin, "Expatriate Labor and Economic Growth."

3. Earlier estimates by two of the authors computed q for 1963–70 at 0.91, for 1970–75 at 0.69, and for 1975–79 at 0.63; see Sherbiny and Serageldin, "Expatriate Labor and Economic Growth," table III, p. 230. The present set of figures was more carefully constructed in the light of more extensive research for the period 1963–70 and updated and more reliable information for 1975–80.

4. Nicholas Kaldor, *Strategic Factors in Economic Development* (Ithaca, N.Y.: Cornell University Press, 1967); R. E. Rowthorn, "A Note on Verdoorn's Law," *Economic Journal*, vol. 89 (March 1979), pp. 131–33.

5. Simon Kuznets, *Modern Economic Growth* (New Haven, Conn.: Yale University Press, 1966); Hollis Chenery and Moises Syrquin, *Patterns of Development, 1950–1970* (London: Oxford University Press, 1975).

6. For a fuller discussion of elasticity calculations in the context of planned development of the Saudi economy, see Sherbiny, "Sectoral Employment Projections."

5. Market Institutions and the Work Force

TRADITIONAL SOCIETIES with little or no modernization tend to have age-old institutions and a stationary labor market. This was the situation in Saudi Arabia in the late 1930s when oil was discovered in commercial quantities. The cumulative effects of oil revenues produced significant socioeconomic changes in the 1950s and particularly in the 1960s. In education, technical training, health, urbanization, housing, transportation, communications, and utilities, myriad changes affected the daily lives of the population; they also affected both the quantity and quality of the Saudi labor force. Many institutional changes affecting labor were introduced during that period. They culminated in the promulgation of a progressive labor law in 1969 which the International Labour Office (ILO) helped formulate along modern lines.

The trends set in motion in the 1950s and 1960s were already accelerating in the early 1970s, when substantially increased oil revenues shifted the pace of economic development and structural change, and modernization proceeded at unprecedented rates. As already indicated in chapter 3, the population of urban centers began to grow rapidly, in part because of internal migration, but fundamentally because of inflows of expatriates (see especially table 3-3). Nearly all the indicators of the quantity and quality of the labor force showed major jumps in the 1970s.

A look at the institutional factors operating in 1978 captures that dynamism and conveys the extent to which the once traditional labor market has traveled on the road to modernization. Conceptually, the institutional factors in this chapter pertain to two categories: the main actors in the labor market, and the prevailing practices in this market, as they were in the late 1970s. The main actors are classified to represent the two sides of the market: workers and employers. Although the focus of the study throughout is on Saudi workers, the institutional framework will be incomplete without some reference to expatriates. Employers are subdivided into private and government establishments, to emphasize the importance of both in the Saudi labor market. With regard to the prevailing market practices, four areas will be covered: unemployment compensation, job search, contractual arrangements, and promotion. This coverage will reveal the simultaneous existence of tradition and modernity in the Saudi labor market. The chapter will conclude with an assessment of market opportunities in general, and of female participation in the work force in particular.

Workers

This section covers some of the institutional factors governing the behavior of the work force, whether Saudi or expatriate. First the profiles of the workers are considered, their general work profile, their educational and occupational levels, and their age and length of service. Then workers' preferences and perceptions are discussed, with reference to their relative socioeconomic position, residence and jobs, as well as their financial obligations that could affect their decisions.

Profiles of the Work Force

GENERAL WORK PROFILE. By definition, workers in the establishment sample were working at the time of the survey. The establishment sample, accordingly, did not provide a full picture of labor force participation in Saudi Arabia. For this reason, an additional sample of households (Saudis and expatriates) was studied to gather information about unemployment, sickness, retirement, and the extent of informality in the labor market, for example, the role of self-employment. The findings showed that unemployment was almost nonexistent (less than 2 percent) among the Saudi adults in the household sample. About 5 percent were retired, and an equal proportion were students. This pattern was almost uniform in all regions. By contrast, the expatriate adults in the household sample were almost all (96 percent) currently working, that is, not just the head of household, but other adults as well. Only 4 percent of the expatriate adults in the household sample were not working (retired, studying, about to leave Saudi Arabia, or just arrived). As the study did not attempt to interview female workers, the occupational distribution might be somewhat distorted—but only slightly, since the present female participation in the labor force is relatively low in Saudi Arabia.

A close examination of the employment status of the Saudi respondents revealed an interesting pattern. About 57 percent of household respondents reported working for a "nonrelative" employer, while a sizable 24 percent indicated they were self-employed, and about 5 percent reported working for a relative (about 3 percent did not indicate their status). This large portion of those self-employed and working for relatives (29 percent) indicates the extent of informality in the labor market. Working for a relative seemed to be more frequent (about 12 percent) in the Southern and Northern regions than the rest of the kingdom (less than 5 percent), while working for an employer was highest in the Eastern region (70 percent).

HEALTH. Although the incidence of sickness is not substantial, it is not negligible. About 12 percent of household respondents reported some sickness during the previous twelve months and more than a fourth of them were sick for three or more months. The incidence was slightly higher for public workers and lower for the private establishment workers. Reported sickness was far less among expatriate workers and of relatively short duration. The incidence of sickness figures for Saudi respondents is about the same as in other developing countries and higher than in developed countries. For example, findings for Pakistan showed that about 25 percent of household respondents had some serious disability in 1969. By contrast, findings for the United States showed that only 9 percent had illness for at least one month (1963–65), and 4 percent had severe disability.[1] Clearly, living standards positively affect the state of health of the labor force. One may therefore expect the figures reported for Saudi Arabia to improve considerably in the 1980s.

EDUCATION AND TRAINING. Training and education are some indicators of the potential level of productivity. The concern here is with general characteristics; a more detailed discussion is given in chapter 6. The first observation is that the vast majority (71 percent) of the Saudi work force in the household sample did not have any past training. Among those who did, their training was equally divided among the various levels of skill, that is, managerial, clerical, technical, skilled, and others. The pattern was similar for the Saudi workers in private establishments, where 91 percent did not have any past training. Actually, none reported any past training in both Northern and Southern regions. Of the Saudis in public establishments, 49 percent reported past training and 7 percent reported current training—most in clerical skills, the rest equally divided among managerial, technical, and other skills. It seems that past training was more of a prerequisite for skilled employment in the public sector. About 47 percent of the expatriate workers in public establishments reported past training, while only 35 percent reported the same in the private establishments.

Table 5-1 reproduces table 3-13, which summarized the level of educa-

Table 5-1. *Distribution of Respondents by Educational Level*
(percent)

	Saudi respondents			Non-Saudi respondents		
	Establishment sample		House-hold sample	Establishment sample		House-hold sample
Educational level	Public	Private		Public	Private	
None	19	20	38	9	23	8
Elementary	27	30	22	6	26	17
Secondary/ intermediate	42	34	28	34	29	24
University/post- graduate	13	16	11	48	14	50
Other	—[a]	—[a]	—[a]	1	8	2
Total	100	100	100	100	100	100

a. Less than 1 percent.

tion among Saudis, and extends the information to cover expatriates. As already indicated, a large proportion of the Saudi household respondents did not have any education (38 percent), and 75 percent did not reach the secondary level of education. Smaller proportions of public and private establishment workers did not have any education: 19 percent and 20 percent, respectively. There are apparent differences in the education/ training profiles of expatriate workers. Almost 49 percent of the expatriates in public establishments had at least a university degree. This was similar to the reported pattern for expatriate households, but was much smaller (14 percent) for expatriates in private establishments.

OCCUPATION. The distribution of all workers by current occupation is summarized in table 5-2. Saudi household respondents who work for an employer are distributed among four main occupations—clerical, production and operative labor, service, and professional (in that order). This pattern was similar in all regions except in the North and South, where the largest percentages are in the service category. About 72 percent of Saudi respondents in public establishments reported they were either clerks or production and operative laborers. Among Saudi respondents in private establishments, 95 percent were concentrated in four occupational groups—administrative/managerial, sales, clerical, and production and operative labor.

The occupational distribution of expatriate respondents, also shown in table 5-2, differed from that of the Saudi respondents. Among expatriate

Table 5-2. *Distribution of Occupations among Respondents*
(percent)

	Saudi respondents			Non-Saudi respondents		
	Establishment sample		House-hold sample	Establishment sample		House-hold sample
Occupation	Public	Private		Public	Private	
Professional	10	2	16	30	8	48
Administrative/ managerial	8	30	7	9	4	8
Clerical	44	22	30	25	13	6
Sales	—ᵃ	24	4	2	22	4
Services	7	3	20	4	7	5
Agriculture	1	0	2	3	0	—ᵃ
Production/ operative	28	19	21	27	46	29
Other	2	—ᵃ	0	—ᵃ	0	0
Total	100	100	100	100	100	100

Note: Only those working for an employer were included in this analysis.
a. Less than 0.5 percent.

household respondents who work for employers, almost half reported they were professionals, and approximately 30 percent reported they were production or operative laborers. The pattern was similar in the various regions. The distribution of expatriate respondents in public establishments was similar to their Saudi counterparts, except that more indicated they were professionals and less were clerks. Finally, the distribution of expatriate respondents in private establishments was almost the same as the distribution of their Saudi counterparts, except that the percentage in administrative/managerial occupations was less, while the percentage in production and operative labor was more.

Discussion of the occupational profile of the work force becomes more meaningful if it is traced over time. The present chapter classifies occupations into three levels: high, medium, and low, to reflect the type of formal qualifications usually required for job entry. High-level occupations refer to professionals and managers/administrators; medium-level occupations refer to clerical, sales, and service workers; and low-level occupations refer to farmers, fishermen, craftsmen, and laborers. Admittedly, such a classification is imperfect and will not meet with universal acceptance, but it remains suitable for the purposes of this discussion. The occupational composition thus highlighted will be discussed on the basis of two sources: the population census of 1974 and findings of the

1978 survey. Strict comparability of these two sources is not possible because the occupational composition according to the census includes workers in the farm sector, while the present study focuses for the most part on nonfarm sectors. For this reason, calculation of the occupational composition from the census was adjusted to exclude farmers.

On this basis, table 5-3 shows that a preponderant share of expatriates in 1974 held low-level occupations while a minor share held high-level occupations. The occupational composition of Saudis in the same year, by contrast, showed about equal shares of low- and medium-level occupations, and a similarly minor share of high-level occupations. By 1978, after many fundamental changes, the occupational composition of both groups shifted dramatically. For the Saudis, the shares of high- and medium-level occupational categories increased at the expense of the low level. For expatriates, high-level occupations became the dominant category, evidently at the expense of the shares of the other two categories. Thus, in 1978 the emerging occupational pattern of expatriate labor complemented the developing occupational composition of Saudi labor more fully than in 1974. The logical inference of increased shares of high-level occupations among Saudi and expatriate workers is that much of the development of, and structural transformation in, the Saudi economy from 1974 to 1978 embodied higher-level technologies.

LENGTH OF EMPLOYMENT. Length of employment is a rough indicator of both the turnover rate and the market's ability to create new opportunities. A summary of the year in which various workers started with their current employers is given in table 5-4. Among Saudi household respondents who work for an employer, more than half have been with their current employer for at least eight years (since 1970 or before). Only 19

Table 5-3. *Occupational Composition of Saudi and Non-Saudi Labor, 1974 and 1978*
(percent)

Occupa-tional level	Saudi		Non-Saudi	
	1974	1978	1974	1978
High	12.2	23.1	13.8	55.5
Medium	43.3	53.8	33.2	15.8
Low	44.5	23.1	53.0	28.7

Sources: Figures for 1974 from Ministry of Finance and National Economy, Central Department of Statistics, *Population Census, 1394 AH* (Riyadh, n.d.) after excluding farmers; 1978 figures from original computer tape of this study (weighted).

Table 5-4. *Distribution of Respondents by Starting Year of Current Job*
(percent)

| Starting year | Saudi respondents | | | Non-Saudi respondents, establishment sample | |
| | Establishment sample | | Household sample | | |
	Public	Private		Public	Private
1977 or after	18	23	9	38	52
1976	10	27	10	16	22
1971–75	34	29	24	21	18
1970 or before	38	21	57	25	8
Total	100	100	100	100	100

percent started work in 1976 or after. This pattern is quite different from that for Saudi establishment respondents, especially in the private sector. In public establishments 38 percent of Saudi respondents have been employed for eight or more years, while 28 percent started in 1976 or after. Even fewer Saudi respondents in private establishments started with their current employer eight or more years ago (21 percent), while 50 percent started in 1976 or after. This pattern of recent employment in the establishment samples was likely to have been the result of expansion in the Saudi economy during the late 1970s, especially in urban areas; it is also compatible with the pattern of recent expansion in private establishment activities.

If demand was creating new opportunities, the turnover rate would be expected to be fast—given supply conditions. Accordingly, a possible index for the response of employment to change in demand was the length of current employment for non-Saudis, especially since for most of them their current employment was their first in the kingdom. Among the non-Saudi respondents in private establishments, a little more than half started during 1977 or after, and another 22 percent in 1976. Only a few (8 percent) have been in their current jobs for eight or more years. The pattern for non-Saudi respondents in the public sector was almost the same except that a larger percentage (25 percent) have been in their current jobs for eight or more years. The short duration of employment might have been the result of contract constraints coupled with fast turnover.

AGE. Dividing the work force into five age groups, as in table 5-5, shows the age profile. At the low end of the profile, below 25 years of age,

Table 5-5. *Age Distribution of Respondents*
(percent)

	Saudis			Non-Saudis		
	Establishment sample		House-hold sample	Establishment sample		House-hold sample
Age	Public	Private		Public	Private	
Under 25	13	20	11	5	16	6
25–34	33	30	23	33	51	28
35–44	33	37	24	26	24	40
45–54	21	11	24	36	7	23
55 +	0	2	18	0	2	3
Total	100	100	100	100	100	100

the work force members are in the start-up phase of their experience, while at the high end, 55 years and older, they are toward the end of their careers. The most productive years are those between 25 and 54. The household sample showed Saudis to be equally distributed within the highly productive range, with a total of 71 percent, and tapering off at both ends. The same sample showed expatriates to be highly concentrated in the 35–44 age category, the prime age for managerial and professional skills, and suddenly falling at both ends of the distribution. The highly productive range encompasses 91 percent of the expatriates. Variations are noted for both Saudis and expatriates in the establishment sample, as noted in table 5-5.

Workers' Preferences and Perceptions

In a rapidly changing environment, social change affects, and is affected by, individual behavior. Such behavioral interaction is not automatic. On the one hand, social change creates new opportunities and choices for individuals in work and in life styles. On the other, individuals are constrained by established norms and value systems, among other things. The result of such interaction is an apparent conflict between the old codes of behavior and the new ways and opportunities. For example, social mobility occurs through either geographical mobility (chapter 8) or occupational mobility (chapter 9). This mobility depends on several factors: the expected net economic gains, the receptivity of individuals to change, their willingness to take risks, and their preferences for types of work or areas of residence, that is, their general attitudes.

How members of the labor force change their attitudes and evaluate, accept, or reject new ways of doing things is an important question. The answers are essential for the understanding of labor market dynamics and for planning purposes—for example, the development of adequate market incentives. But it is also a difficult question because attitudes are multidimensional and shape social behavior in possibly conflicting ways. The purpose here is to examine some of the noneconomic factors that influence the adjustment process in the Saudi labor market.

PERCEPTION OF RELATIVE SOCIOECONOMIC POSITION. Satisfaction with the current situation may indicate occupational fulfillment, an excess of income over needs, acceptance of whatever happens, or a combination of such factors. In the study, an attempt was made to measure the workers' evaluation of their own conditions and achievements. Workers were asked whether they felt their previous year's income was adequate for their needs; how their earnings compared with those of others in similar jobs; whether they had had better-paying jobs in the past; and finally, whether they were making adequate use of their education and training in their current jobs.

On the question of adequacy of income, it seems that almost all Saudi workers felt their previous year's income was at least adequate (95–99 percent). A sizable proportion felt that it was "much more than adequate." When asked to compare their own earnings with those of others, however, a significant proportion were uncertain or felt it was worse (16 percent and 20 percent in the case of Saudi households and private establishment workers, respectively). A much larger portion (39 percent) were uncertain or dissatisfied among the Saudi workers in public establishments. The non-Saudi sample indicates a similar pattern.

In some cases Saudi workers had had better-paying jobs in the past: about 11 percent of those in public establishments but only 5 percent of those in private establishments. However, the vast majority of both Saudi and non-Saudi workers did not experience a loss of pay. Finally, there is a general sense of accomplishment among the Saudi labor force. Less than 5 percent indicated that their jobs do not adequately use their education and training. There were some regional differences: in the North more of the Saudi respondents in private establishments and households felt that their training and education were not adequately utilized.

PLACE OF RESIDENCE. To some extent, satisfaction with the present place of residence increases the perceived cost of moving. Three types of attitude toward place of residence are examined: residents' satisfaction with the school system in their locality, their preferences for working in a given region, and their preferences for living in that region.

The findings showed that the majority of Saudi respondents were satisfied with their current place of residence: 86 percent in private establishments, 82 percent in households, and 72 percent in public establishments. Among those indicating dissatisfaction, the most frequent cause was related to a crowded neighborhood, followed by the uncertainty of tenure when, for example, a rental agreement had expired or a lease had been terminated. Among the non-Saudi respondents, an even larger majority were satisfied with their current residence; among those dissatisfied, the main reason was also overcrowding.

The school system did not seem to be a source of dissatisfaction. About 90 percent of the Saudi households were satisfied with the system in their locality—the majority (41 percent) because of the quality of the curriculum, and 20 percent because of the facilities and environment of the school. The pattern is essentially the same for the Saudi establishment workers, as well as for non-Saudi respondents.

When asked which region they preferred to work in, many respondents indicated no preference (41 percent and 38 percent of Saudi workers in public and private establishments, respectively). There was, however, an apparent preference for *avoiding* the Southern region. Even among Southern residents, a significant proportion indicated their dislike of working in that region. Interestingly, there was no clear preference among Saudi respondents for or against the sparsely populated Northern region, which the central government is trying to develop as one of the country's "new frontiers."

OCCUPATIONAL PREFERENCES. For unclear historical, or perhaps even accidental, reasons, various occupations and types of jobs have acquired prestige. The pattern of occupational preferences could influence relative wages and potential mobility among occupations. Respondents were asked a set of questions to examine their motivation and attitudes. First, they were asked in which industry they preferred to work. Second, they were asked to rank sectors according to the most preferred and the least preferred. Finally, they were asked to rank certain job characteristics.

Saudi respondents in all three samples showed a decided preference for the social and personal service sector (at least 40 percent in each of the three samples). A smaller but significant percentage (about 20 percent in each of the three samples) indicated a preference for the manufacturing sector. Among Saudi respondents in the public sector, there was some preference (17 percent) for agriculture, hunting, and mining and quarrying. Little preference was shown by these respondents for the remaining sectors.

Among the non-Saudi household respondents, about 31 percent indicated preference for work in the social and personal service sector. Equal proportions (14–15 percent each) indicated preference for manufacturing, construction, wholesale and retail, and finance. None indicated preference for the utilities sector (electricity, gas, and water) and very few for transportation and agriculture.

When asked to rank jobs according to their preference, Saudi respondents gave highest score to jobs in sales and trade, in the oil industry, and in government (table 5-6). Interestingly, relatively more Saudi respondents in public establishments ranked government first (52 percent) and sales and trade relatively low. Construction, banking, and army and police jobs seem to have a relatively low ranking among Saudi respondents, as indicated by the frequency of first rank. The low ranking assigned to banking as compared with sales and trade may reflect the relatively recent establishment of the banking industry, even though it is rapidly expanding, as well as its clerical image.

To explore some of the factors underlying job preference, respondents were given a set of five job characteristics—security, income, prestige, promotion, and location—and were asked to rank them according to which they considered most important when deciding on a job. The percentage of respondents ranking each of these characteristics as the most important in selecting a job are shown in table 5-7. Security and income are the most important, while prestige, promotion, and location are the least important job characteristics. Respondents in public estab-

Table 5-6. *Occupational Preferences, by Sector*
(percentage of respondents giving first rank)

	Saudi respondents			Non-Saudi respondents		
	Establishment sample		House-hold sample	Establishment sample		House-hold sample
Sector	*Public*	*Private*		*Public*	*Private*	
Government	55	33	49	40	30	35
Banking	2	4	3	16	8	9
Sales/trade	8	26	24	10	28	16
Army/police	6	7	12	3	2	3
Oil industry	24	20	5	13	5	8
Manufacturing	8	11	5	18	19	20
Construction	0	4	6	3	14	20

Note: Columns may add up to more than 100 because of multiple mentions.

Table 5-7. *Most Important Job Characteristics*
(percentage of respondents giving first rank)

	Saudi respondents			Non-Saudi respondents		
	Establishment sample		House-hold sample	Establishment sample		House-hold sample
Charac-teristic	Public	Private		Public	Private	
Security	48	32	43	62	40	36
Income	31	45	32	25	42	46
Prestige	5	10	6	7	5	9
Promotion	10	3	5	2	2	2
Location	6	10	13	5	6	6

lishments, whether Saudis or non-Saudis, rank security first (48 percent and 62 percent, respectively). By working for public establishments, those individuals have already revealed a preference for job security. Interestingly, however, while security ranked above income among Saudi households, it ranked below income among non-Saudi households. Furthermore, income ranked ahead of security among workers in private establishments, regardless of nationality—a sign of receptivity to market incentives.

FINANCIAL OBLIGATIONS. One of the influences on motivation and attitudes toward work and taking risks is the perception of future obligations and commitments. Conservative attitudes could increase the cost of mobility and lead to a preference for jobs that provide security as opposed to advancement and growth. About half the Saudi household workers indicated that they had financial obligations, mostly to their children and their family. This was also true for an even larger proportion of the public establishment sample (79 percent) and the private establishment sample (65 percent). The main obligations cited were education and marriage for the household sample; for the establishment sample, education and "general expenses."

Employers

This section focuses on the other side of the labor market, the institutional factors governing the demand for labor. The analysis will cover two types of employers: public and private establishments. To place employers in the proper context, the discussion starts with an overview of the institutional role of government in the labor market (that is, its jurisdiction over labor affairs and responsibility for maintenance of labor legislation) before proceeding to the role of government as an employer. An examination of the job benefits offered by public and private establishments concludes this section.

Government Role in the Labor Market

JURISDICTION OVER LABOR AFFAIRS. The Ministry of Labor and Social Affairs was established in 1961 as the official government agency concerned with labor. The ministry was reorganized in 1970 and 1971 into two major branches, the Directorate for Labor Affairs and the Directorate for Social Affairs, to provide more effective services to workers and employers. The Directorate for Labor Affairs is responsible for regulations including labor inspection, safety provisions, settlement of disputes, and compliance with the requirements for social services for workers. It operates vocational training centers and apprenticeship programs. The centralized structure functions on a regional basis through twenty-eight labor offices, four of which are regional (in the East, Center, West, and South). The labor offices perform several functions, free of charge, including registration and placement of job applicants, maintenance of records and job transfers, and review of applications from expatriates for work and residence permits.

The labor directorate in Saudi Arabia assumes many of the responsibilities which labor unions carry in more industrialized countries. The government takes a strong paternalistic and protective approach to labor, as evidenced by 1969 legislation giving the Ministry of Labor broad powers to regulate labor and social services. Government supervision and regulation of labor affairs in private industry has developed gradually; it started with the oil companies and large foreign contractors, and has extended to large local firms.

The Directorate for Social Affairs operates largely at the regional level. The plan defines social services to labor as including, but not being limited to, medical care, safety precautions, housing, recreational facilities, transportation, meal services, retail purchase arrangements, and a savings system.

Overseeing labor affairs in government, including labor allocations among various branches and entities, is the Civil Service Board. The board carries out the government's employment policy, which seeks to develop the required number of properly qualified individuals to staff planned projects.

LABOR LEGISLATION. The 1969 labor law is the cornerstone of the maintenance, development, and well-being of labor in Saudi Arabia. To protect workers it requires employers to honor contracts as binding commitments. Employers cannot sever workers' contracts unilaterally without resorting to the labor offices or to courts. Severance pay is calculated on the basis of the last salary in cases such as expiration or discontinuation of contract, military service, and marriage or birth in the case of female workers. Wages are protected and payments are made at regular intervals, monthly or weekly. No deductions from wages can be made without the worker's permission. Acquired rights of the workers are irrevocable. Health care is the responsibility of the employer, especially in establishments with more than fifty employees. Special provisions protect youths (13–18 years) against exploitation and provide for physical and psychological comfort for women workers.

The maximum number of working hours per day is eight (in Ramadan, six), with a maximum of six days a week. Overtime is limited to ten hours a week at 150 percent times the regular hourly pay. Annual vacations are fifteen days at full pay for workers with less than ten years of service, and twenty-one days for workers with ten years or more of service. Sick leave is thirty days a year at full pay plus sixty days at three-quarters pay for large and medium establishments.

Social services—transportation, voluntary savings, and recreational facilities—are the responsibility of the employers. Mining employers must provide, in addition, suitable housing, three meals a day, health, and social and cultural services. Especially large employers (those with more than 500 employees), and depending on their location, are required by law to provide shops for food and clothing, parks, sports activities, medical services, schools for children, mosques, and literacy programs.

Full formal machinery for hearing labor-management disputes was created in 1970 in accordance with the 1969 law. Government and management had preferred in the past to settle disputes informally, in harmony with the social and religious traditions of Islam. This method, however, could not meet the complex needs of labor in large enterprises. The present procedure calls for initial consideration of labor disputes in Primary Commissions, followed by appeal to a Supreme Commission if no satisfactory resolution is reached. Primary Commissions are attached to local and regional labor offices.

Government as Employer

Not only does the government play a central role in the Saudi economy, it is also a principal employer. In 1970, government employment was 17 percent of total civilian nonfarm employment. In 1975, despite the rapid expansion in nonfarm employment, government employment was still significant—more than 15 percent. Government impact, however, is even greater than these figures suggest, because of public and semipublic enterprises in the various "private" sectors: crude oil and oil manufacturing, utilities, finance, transport, and communications. The present analysis does not distinguish between government administration employment and public sector employment.

Government employment offers attractive conditions such as short work hours, acceptable salaries, generous vacation and sick leave, security of tenure, scholarships abroad and at home, training incentives, and a pension plan. Employment in government attracts highly qualified professionals and carries prestige at most levels, especially for white-collar workers. For these reasons, a large proportion of Saudis prefer the public sector, as evidenced by their indicated preferences in ranking government jobs. For example, about 70 percent of the respondents in the household sample gave first or second ranking to government jobs.

Government employment policy in the public sector is carried out by the Civil Service Board, which was recently reorganized to render its service more efficient. It attempts to allocate labor to the various branches of government in a centralized fashion. The rationale is that only when the board has an overview of labor resources and uses as well as shifts in these variables over time can it allocate new labor increments efficiently. For this reason, the board regularly monitors the education system's supply of skills as well as the skill requirements of government branches. The board applies one set of rules to both Saudis and expatriates in public sector employment, but gives a preference to Saudis, especially at the higher levels. For positions which no Saudi can fill, the board arranges for the employment of expatriates.

To upgrade the quality of employed labor in the public sector, the government started the Institute of Public Administration in 1961. The institute provides training to a wide range of public sector employees (Saudis only) from top management to clerical levels. In 1971 the institute started a two-year program to prepare candidates for civil service in a variety of public fields such as administration, public finance, customs, and statistics. The number of trainees at the institute increased from 1,000 a year in 1971 to 5,000 in 1978, and it is planned to train significantly more than that during the 1980s. The implications of such plans for the labor market may go beyond the confines of the public sector, since many of the trainees may end up in the private sector.

Despite these efforts, the government sector has coped only partly with the demands of its branches for various skills. Obstacles such as the need for administrative reorganization to redistribute responsibilities, for the delegation of authority, and for comprehensive manpower planning impede the centralization of employment policy. For these reasons, the government cannot adequately synchronize output flows of the education system with the development requirements for human resources. Indicative of the problem is that some levels and branches of government have become increasingly overstaffed, while others, such as health services, continue to be seriously understaffed because of the lack of skilled personnel. One example at the national level is that there were 235,000 jobs in the 1975–76 government budget, but only 189,000 jobs were filled, a shortfall of 46,000, or a vacancy rate of 20 percent.

Contributing to the severity of the vacancy problem in government employment is the keen competition for qualified persons from the private sector. This is particularly noticeable in high and middle administrative positions. In 1972 the U.S. Department of Labor issued a report on labor conditions in Saudi Arabia which stated that "some young men have been lured away from government employment by better opportunities, especially in commerce and blue-collar employment in the petroleum industry."[2] Although this trend has continued to the present, Saudis still constitute the majority in public sector employment, in contrast to the situation in the private sector. According to this study's findings, Saudis constitute 57 percent of public sector employment, compared with 23 percent in small private establishments and 14 percent in large private establishments.

Job Benefits

Employment benefits constitute an important component of total compensation to labor, although frequently excluded from reported regular pay. Not all such benefits can be easily measured. For example, work location and environment may enter workers' valuation of total job benefits. This section presents the distribution of the various types of job benefits among the Saudi and non-Saudi labor in public and private establishments for the various regions.

Respondents were asked whether their employers provide for eight specific job benefits: annual leave, sick leave, health insurance, disability benefits, free accommodation or allowance for housing, transport allowance, training benefits, and allowance for child education. A summary of the findings for Saudis and non-Saudis is presented in table 5-8.

For the Saudi household respondents, annual leave is a common benefit (86 percent), followed by sick leave (76 percent), transportation allowance (58 percent), health insurance (40 percent), and disability benefits (30 percent). Only 15 percent of the Saudi respondents in the

Table 5-8. *Job Benefits*
(percentage of respondents citing benefit)

	Saudi respondents			Non-Saudi respondents		
	Establishment sample		House-hold sample	Establishment sample		House-hold sample
Benefit	Public	Private		Public	Private	
Annual leave	80	90	86	100	77	86
Sick leave	74	78	76	52	56	43
Health insurance	79	67	40	58	48	38
Disability benefits	65	41	25	36	26	9
Housing	10	23	15	76	47	66
Transportation	82	32	58	80	28	44
Training	16	6	4	0	1	2
Children's education	1	3	1	4	0	0
Other	13	4	4	12	5	6

Note: Columns do not add up to 100 because of multiple mentions.

household sample were provided with a housing subsidy. Provisions for training and allowance for child education are not common job benefits for Saudis in the labor market. They were reported by less than 5 percent of the working population.

A comparison of benefits between the household sample and establishment sample (public and private) indicates no systematic difference in general. There are, however, differences between public and private establishments. For example, the public sector provides a larger transportation allowance (82 percent compared with 32 percent), more of the respondents in the public sector indicated training as a benefit (16 percent versus 6 percent), while few indicated provision of housing subsidy (10 percent versus 23 percent). Furthermore, a comparison between Saudi and non-Saudi workers indicates that benefits were generally larger for the Saudis. The only exceptions were housing allowances and, to a lesser extent, annual leave.

Market Practices

Having reviewed the institutional factors affecting the behavior of the actors on both sides of the labor market, the discussion turns to the practices most prevalent in the Saudi market, as they emerged from the survey findings. Four major aspects are discussed: unemployment compensation, the process of job search, contractual arrangements, and promotion.

Unemployment Compensation

In 1970, unemployment in Saudi Arabia was estimated by the U.S. Department of Labor at about 6 percent.[3] Eight years later, after considerable changes in the size and structure of the Saudi labor market, the present study estimated unemployment at 2 percent. The proportion of respondents who had ever experienced unemployment was not considerable. Among Saudi household respondents, about 10 percent had ever been unemployed, and most of them had been unemployed only once (8 percent). Among the establishment workers, the incidence of reported past unemployment was even lower (less than 6 percent). The picture was not different for the non-Saudi respondents. The highest incidence of ever experiencing unemployment was reported by those in the public sector (12 percent), while it was less than 6 percent for the others. When examining their most recent unemployment experience, most of the Saudi respondents indicated private means as their major source of financial support during that period (for example, savings or parents and relatives), typical of developing countries. Two sources of funds, unemployment compensation and formal borrowing, were not used, which is in line with traditional values. The same pattern was essentially true for non-Saudi respondents.

Noteworthy in these findings is the incidence of ever experiencing unemployment among expatriates. The reason for expatriates to be in Saudi Arabia is work. In fact, expatriates are not granted entry visas unless they have either jobs or a *Kafeel* (Saudi sponsor). The law requires expatriates to leave the country if their relations with either employers or Kafeels are terminated. The location of unemployment among expatriates was not reported, however—that is, whether the unemployment had occurred in Saudi Arabia or in the country of origin, before coming to Saudi Arabia. If unemployment had been experienced in the country of origin, this would have been a strong incentive to seek employment in Saudi Arabia. If it had been experienced in Saudi Arabia, it would indicate that the job market was sufficiently fluid to allow expatriates to move between jobs or even change Kafeels (frictional unemployment) without leaving the country.

The Process of Job Search

What are the most frequent methods of recruitment in the Saudi labor market? Methods could be divided rather arbitrarily into formal and informal. For example, personal contacts or direct "walk-in" may be considered informal methods, as compared with more formal recruitment through employment agencies, consultant firms, mass media, or recruiting missions and government agreements (mainly for expatriate labor). When asked the method of finding their most recent *previous* jobs, most Saudi respondents (over 85 percent) indicated either personal contacts or walk-in, and 79 percent of Saudi workers in private establishments reported personal contact alone. It seems that most of the recruiting was done somewhat informally. The mass media were reported by less than 5 percent of the Saudi labor force, not a surprising finding in view of the high illiteracy among Saudi respondents.

The picture was somewhat different for the non-Saudi respondents. Although the two informal methods (personal contacts and walk-in) accounted together for the majority of reported recruiting methods (between 50 and 70 percent), the mass media accounted for a larger proportion than it did for the Saudis, especially in public establishments. Government agreements and recruiting missions did not seem to play a major role at that time. Did the situation change recently?

The job search methods employed to locate *current* jobs were not different from before. The majority of Saudi workers (between 76 and 96 percent) indicated walk-in and personal contacts as their methods, which was similar to the previous findings. The only difference seems to have been greater use of the media (12 percent and 14 percent for household heads and workers in public establishments, respectively, compared with 5 percent reported above). Another observation is the relatively more frequent use of government agreements in the Northern and Southern regions. Otherwise, not much change occurred over time. The process of job recruiting remains mostly informal. The same conclusion could be drawn regarding non-Saudi workers.

Because workers were recruited at different times, a more accurate picture of current practice was given by the methods selected by those planning to change their jobs at the time of the survey and looking for another one. The proportion of the labor force looking for another job was less than 16 percent. It was lowest for non-Saudi respondents in the household sample and highest for the Saudi respondents also in the household sample.

The method of job search for those workers at present looking for another job is summarized in table 5-9. It is evident that the Saudi labor market is still essentially informal. Note the low figure for the use of mass media even among those employed in government, who would have been expected to rely more on formal approaches. There is, however, relatively greater use of the mass media than previously, especially to recruit foreign labor.

Contractual Arrangements

The provision of a contract for a stated duration could have both positive and negative effects for both employers and employees. In the case of a labor shortage, especially when long-term growth is expected, it is beneficial for employers to attempt to bind their workers for relatively long periods. But if employers are likely to be faced with fluctuations in market conditions, it would be to their advantage to have less contractual rigidity; for example, so that they could lay off workers when necessary. The workers' preference for contractual rigidity will depend largely on whether they are Saudi or non-Saudi. For Saudis, it will not be advantageous to be bound with long-term contracts, especially when the market is expanding and opportunities improving. The situation is different for non-Saudis. Faced with institutional constraints on changing jobs within Saudi Arabia, they will tend to prefer contractual arrangements which are binding to employers in terms of duration. Thus, it was ex-

Table 5-9. *Methods Used to Search for Current Job*
(percentage of respondents)

Method of job search	Saudi respondents			Non-Saudi respondents		
	Establishment sample		House-hold sample	Establishment sample		House-hold sample
	Public	Private		Public	Private	
Through friend	48	59	54	25	68	68
Through media	3	20	10	5	25	37
Employment agency	0	6	7	4	21	6
Walk-in	27	22	33	54	50	33
Labor office	1	2	4	3	18	0
Other	25	12	20	12	11	7

Note: Column percentages may add up to more than 100 because of multiple mentions.

pected that Saudi respondents would have fewer contractual arrangements than non-Saudis, and the findings do support this a priori assessment.

Almost all Saudi household respondents expectedly did *not* have a contract (over 95 percent). This picture is quite different for the non-Saudi household respondents, about 70 percent of whom indicated having contractual arrangements, and 50 percent for a duration of two or more years. The pattern was similar for the non-Saudi respondents in the private and public sectors, but with relatively more contractual arrangement in the public sector (82 percent in public and 56 percent in private). In situations involving no formal contractual arrangements, it would be difficult for the regional labor offices to resolve conflicts between workers and employers.

Although the proportion of Saudi respondents with contracts was very low, it is useful to examine for those who had a contract whether their contract would end in the current year or would be renewed. The findings show that all Saudi workers with a contract indicated their contract either would not end or, if it was to end, would be renewed. The picture was essentially the same for non-Saudis in the public sector. For non-Saudis in the private sector, about 2 percent said they had other jobs or would have training, 4 percent indicated they would return home, and 3 percent would be looking for a job. The majority (89 percent) said either their contract would not end (63 percent) or would be renewed (26 percent).

Promotion

In general, promotion (including higher pay) is expected to be common in a growing economy. For some workers, the presence of advancement possibilities, objectively or subjectively, could be an important criterion for the choice of a job. Respondents were first asked if they had been promoted. If they gave affirmative answers, they were then asked about the type of promotion they had experienced. In this regard, although promotion may be objectively identified, it was the respondents' perception which was being sought. Findings indicated that promotion thus defined had been more prevalent among Saudi workers in public establishments (70 percent) than among those working in private establishments (25 percent). The most important types of promotion in the public sector were "new title" (39 percent) and "more responsibility" (22 percent). In the private sector, more responsibility was the most frequently mentioned type of promotion by Saudi workers (13 percent). Essentially, this same pattern of promotion was reported by Saudi household respondents. Just over half have been promoted. For these workers, the promotion has meant either more responsibility (19 percent), or a new title (17 percent) or an increase in salary (11 percent). This general pattern did not differ significantly among regions.

In the case of non-Saudis, the pattern was entirely different. Most non-Saudis (in all three samples) have not been promoted; for example, the maximum portion promoted in the sample of private establishments was approximately 25 percent. For non-Saudis in the public establishment and household samples, the proportion was less than 25 percent. The few that have been promoted received either higher salaries or new titles.

Conclusions

This chapter attempted to describe and analyze the institutional framework of the Saudi labor market by using two sources: available data and published information prior to 1978, and the findings of the 1978 field survey underlying the present study. The chapter portrayed the actors on both sides of the market—the workers and employers—and described the practices emanating from the interaction of those two groups. The picture that emerges is predictably complex, one of a society in the midst of a rapid and far-reaching transition from tradition to modernity, and of a labor market in the process of transformation from relative stability to dynamism. Elements of extreme disparity appear side by side to make the labor market of Saudi Arabia all the more enigmatic and especially fascinating for students of economics and sociology.

The outcome of those conflicting trends and contradictory forces is nowhere better manifested than in the market opportunities in general and female employment in particular. One mark of efficiency is the ability of the market to transmit information regarding current and potential job opportunities to the various segments of the labor force. If workers have up-to-date knowledge about job possibilities and alternatives, they can improve their market opportunities and make better use of their abilities and skills. In addition, employers are able to hire the best workers for the jobs available. As a result, the labor market becomes more competitive and efficient. Such an ideal situation does not exist. Usually deviations from that ideal cause losses to workers and employers alike. Examples include considerable informality in the practices of labor hiring; less than full information about available job opportunities; and, more generally, selective information for specific segments of the labor force. Such imperfections in the network of labor market information could weaken the response of either labor supply (via geographic and occupational mobility) or labor demand (output growth and structural change). As background, the following questions were examined: Why did workers leave their previous jobs? Did they have a meaningful choice of job alternatives?

As already noted, for many Saudis (50 percent in private and public establishments, 63 percent among household respondents), their current job was their first. For those who had had a previous job, the majority indicated that the reason for leaving was either that they found a better job or that their previous job paid inadequately. This pattern was the same for the private and public establishment sample and for the household sample. Very few indicated being fired as a reason for leaving their previous jobs (less than 8 percent), although a sizable proportion (ranging from 25–57 percent) had other undefined reasons. The picture for non-Saudi workers is essentially the same. Most non-Saudi respondents indicated low salary or finding a better job as the leading two reasons for leaving the recent employment. The question then raised was to what extent workers had a choice when they decided to accept their current job offer.

All workers were asked whether they had alternative job offers to choose from at the time of deciding on their current job. The majority of Saudi workers (more than 75 percent) indicated that they had no job alternatives. However, 26 percent of Saudi household respondents who were currently employed (not self-employed) indicated that they had an alternative job offer. The proportion was 24 percent for Saudi workers in public establishments and only 14 percent for those in private establishments. The proportion of non-Saudi respondents who had alternative job offers from which to choose was essentially the same.

The processes of urbanization and modernization have inevitably pushed forward the importance of female education. The explosive growth in female education noted in chapter 3 is but a manifestation of the potential role of women in the work force. Saudi traditions prohibit women from mixing with men in the workplace. This, however, should not be interpreted to mean that there is no place for women in the work force. The growing dynamism of the Saudi society is creating significant opportunities for female employment, especially in education, family and health care, and selected other occupations. To assess the receptivity to such developments, respondents were asked about their attitude toward female employment.

The majority (57 percent) of Saudi household respondents approved of females working. This proportion was lowest in the Northern region (30 percent) but highest in the Eastern region (68 percent). It was higher yet among public establishment workers (74 percent). Among private establishment workers, however, the proportion was only 51 percent. When asked about the circumstances under which females may hold a job, about 27 percent of Saudi heads of household said under no circumstances. So did 10 percent of private establishment workers, and 16 percent of public establishment workers. About 44 percent of household respondents, however, indicated females could work if in financial need, 12 percent if they were single, widowed, or with no male relative, and only 5 percent made it unconditional.

Despite the sweeping changes in the economy and labor market of Saudi Arabia, members of the Saudi labor force still maintain a traditional outlook, as manifested by the strong preferences expressed for their residential locations, job security, and public sector employment; by the strong financial and social commitment to family; and by the qualified approval of female employment. This traditional outlook, however, is itself in a state of flux as a consequence of the rapidly changing environment and the constant introduction of new work and life styles. Further adjustments will undoubtedly be made by the present generation of Saudis. In this sense, Saudi Arabia is not alone among developing societies in facing the dilemmas of modernization, although the Saudi experience is undoubtedly much more accelerated.

Notes

1. For Pakistan, see Johns Hopkins University, "Pakistan National Impact Survey," First Report (Baltimore, Md., 1971; processed); for the United States, see James N. Morgan, Ismail A. Sirageldin, and Nancy Baerwaldt, *Productive Americans* (Ann Arbor, Mich.: University of Michigan Press, 1966).

2. U.S. Department of Labor, Bureau of Labor Statistics, *Labor Law and Practice in the Kingdom of Saudi Arabia*, BLS Report no. 407 (Washington, D.C.: U.S. Government Printing Office, 1973), p. 42.

3. Bureau of Labor Statistics, *Labor Law and Practice*.

6. Skill Formation

CHAPTER 3 CLEARLY DISTINGUISHED between the quantitative aspects of labor supply and its qualitative aspects as measured by literacy and education, loosely grouped under the heading of skill formation. The present chapter takes a closer look at the question of skill formation.

Looming large in the background is the extent of illiteracy among the Saudi work force. Any effort to develop skills in Saudi Arabia must start by considering the extent of national literacy. As mentioned in chapter 3, the picture which emerged from the 1974 census was sobering: 52 percent of Saudi men and 79 percent of Saudi women were illiterate. When this overall picture is broken down by age-specific groups, however, there are some bright spots: each age group, male or female, was more literate than the next older one. The case was particularly striking for young males entering the job market: their illiteracy rates were about half those of their fathers' generation (table 3-4).

Having been long aware of these facts, the government spared no efforts not only in expanding education, but also in combating illiteracy. Large programs of adult education were launched as early as the 1960s, but became especially massive during the 1970s. The statistics are revealing. In 1964–65, the government was managing 393 schools with 1,172 classes to combat illiteracy and educate about 33,000 adults. By 1979–80, the adult education program had extended to 3,357 schools with 9,334 classes serving 142,000 adults (see table 3-8).

Fundamentally for this reason, when the field survey of the present study was conducted in 1978, the literacy results showed significant improvements over the 1974 census. The questions specifically aimed at assessing "functional illiteracy" among respondents (all males). For the purposes of the survey, functional illiteracy was defined as lack of ability to read and write or to perform simple mathematical calculations (add, subtract, multiply, and divide). The target group for the functional illiteracy test were those in the household sample who had either no formal education or only elementary education. Although the same tests were conducted among the worker sample, the household sample is more representative of the Saudi population. As table 3-13 showed, 38 percent of the Saudi household sample had no formal education, while 22 percent had only elementary education. The target group as a whole thus comprised 60 percent of the Saudi households. When respondents in the target group were asked whether they could read or write, 41 percent answered no. This implies that about 24 percent of *all* Saudi household respondents were illiterate (41 percent of 60). In regard to the numeracy test, 45 percent of the respondents in the target group said they could not add, and slightly more said they could not subtract, multiply, or divide. This means that about 27 percent of *all* Saudi household respondents were numerically illiterate (45 percent of 60).

Just because an individual can read or write does not, of course, mean that he can perform adequately in a modernizing society or even meet the daily demands of most unskilled jobs. But the ability to perform simple mathematical calculations seems to be essential in many occupations; without it a worker cannot take measurements, keep financial records, read blueprints, or do several other tasks.

Against this general background this chapter attempts to grapple with the question of skill formation. A rapidly expanding labor market, fueled by accelerated growth of investment and consumption expenditures, calls for both short-term and long-term responses.

Short-term adjustments by the labor force to rapidly changing conditions have to be made either through the inflow of foreign labor to fill gaps in the various skills of the labor market or through a restructuring of the existing stock of Saudi workers, that is, through mobility or training programs. As already noted, since a large segment of the Saudi labor force had little or no formal education and only a small percentage had any training (either on or off the job), the government has committed large amounts of resources for various training programs. The utilization of these services will depend both on their supply and on the demand for them among the Saudi work force. An important question accordingly is the extent of Saudi participation in training activities and the factors that determine their participation.

In the long run, however, attention must be given not only to the existing stock, but also to the flow of new entrants into the labor market. As mentioned earlier, the government commitment to universal education is constrained only by the time needed to build facilities and acquire trained teachers and administrators. Finance has hitherto been of no concern. Even here, some important questions arise; for example, what are the skill levels and educational profiles of the young Saudi entrants into the labor market? What are their work plans, their aspirations, and their attitude toward work and leisure? The questions are clearly too specific and thus need special and detailed inquiry. In the present chapter, however, the topic is examined only in outline. In the first section, short-run adjustments through training of the current generation are examined. In the second section, the focus will be on the education of the new generation.

In the Short Run

From a developmental perspective, the relative prevalence of illiteracy and the lack of supplementary training among the Saudi labor force raise questions about the basic skills available. This section therefore takes a closer look at training, past and present, and attempts to analyze critically the determinants of current training.

The general objective of training is to improve the average quality of human resources. Several approaches are usually attempted, including specific job-related training and general public education such as for functional literacy. In view of the high priority the government has given to training, the utilization of such services as reported by Saudi respondents is examined here. Training in functional literacy did not reach many of the Saudi household respondents, as evidenced by both the high illiteracy rate and low attendance at literacy classes (5 percent). Of the few who attended, most went to evening classes (76 percent). The average duration of class attendance was more than two years. Employers arranged for literacy training in only 2 percent of the cases; the remainder were arranged either by the government (43 percent) or directly by the individual (46 percent).

In contrast to literacy training, job training aims, in general, to improve performance in specific job activities and to supplement basic skills obtained through the formal education system. First, we examine those who had ever received any job training; second, current participation in such training is discussed. The percentages of workers receiving past and current job training is given in table 6-1.

Past Job Training

As table 6-1 indicates, 22 percent of the Saudi household respondents had received training before taking their current job. The percentage of Saudi workers with past training was substantially higher among those in public establishments and substantially lower in private establishments.

The type of past training of Saudi respondents by skill category is shown in table 6-2. Among the three major types of skill (managerial, clerical, and technical), training was concentrated in clerical skills for

Table 6-1. *Percentage of Respondents with Past and Current Job Training*

	Saudi respondents			Non-Saudi respondents		
	Establishment sample		House-hold sample	Establishment sample		House-hold sample
Job training	Public	Private		Public	Private	
Past	49	8	22	47	35	n.a.
Current	7	1	7	3	11	5

n.a. Not available.

Table 6-2. *Type of Past Training of Saudi Respondents*
(percent)

	Establishment sample		Household sample
Training	Public	Private	
Managerial	16	6	16
Clerical	40	19	20
Technical	23	53	20
Other	21	22	44

public establishment workers and in technical skills for private establishment workers. However, it was more evenly distributed among various skills for households.

More detailed figures, not shown here, indicate that the type of training also varied from one region to the next. In the Central region many respondents across the samples (households and public and private establishments) had received managerial training; in the Eastern region, technical training; in the Western region, clerical training. In the Northern and Southern regions none of the Saudi workers in private establishments had received prior training.

Saudi respondents who had received training were asked to indicate who had arranged and paid for their training. Answers varied across samples. In the household sample past training was usually financed by the government but arranged by the recipient. For workers in the public sector past training was financed and arranged mainly by the government or by other employers, depending on the region in which the worker lived. For public workers in the Eastern and Western regions most financing and arrangements were by employers; in the Central, Northern, and Southern regions it was by the government. Among Saudi workers in private establishments almost all arrangements and payments were made by the employers.

The attitude of Saudis toward prior training was ascertained for respondents in the public and private sectors. Overwhelmingly they agreed that the training was relevant to their current work.

Current Job Training

Table 6-1 also indicates that the percentage of the labor force receiving current training (defined as training received after beginning work for their current employer) was much lower than the percentage of those who had received training in the past. For example, among Saudi workers in public establishments, 49 percent had received training before beginning work for their current employer, while only 7 percent had any training since starting their current job. Because the percentage of respondents receiving current training is so small, it is impossible to establish reliable generalizations about the type of training, its method of financing, and other arrangements.

The present analysis attempts to identify the factors underlying the pattern of current training among Saudis in the labor force. There are a number of questions of interest to manpower policy, especially with regard to maximizing the effectiveness of the job training program: information about who is being trained, especially which educational and age groups, should shed light on the returns (public or private) to such an investment. While the public strategy would be to reach those with minimal or no training, the individual's perspective may differ. Within a human capital framework, the higher the level of education of an individual worker, the lower the relative net return, but the efficiency of assimilating knowledge may increase, and with it the demand for training. Age is probably negatively related to training. The older the worker, the shorter the remaining years, and accordingly the lower the present value of the expected future benefits (other things being equal). The cost of training will be less for individuals in urban areas where facilities are more available and accessible. For those working in the public sector, where training is more systematically organized and in some instances mandatory, the cost of training is almost nonexistent for the individual. The perceived adequacy of the individual's income may be a stronger motivational force than the actual salary level if traditions and relative values still dominate. To test these postulates, we turn next to multivariate analysis of current training of Saudi workers.

There is no reason to expect Saudi workers to respond to training in a predictable pattern within a human capital framework. The sudden surge in demand, the large inflows of expatriate workers, the differential pattern of regional development, and the training subsidies in the public and private sectors make a priori predictions difficult. In the following multivariate analysis the dependent variable is whether the Saudi worker was receiving any training at the time of interview, and there were nine explanatory variables expected to influence workers' decisions to participate in training.

The education variable reflects differential evaluation of the returns to additional training. Higher levels of education indicate both diminishing returns to additional training and better, more efficient utilization of such training—thus higher returns. But in a changing environment, it is possible that those with higher levels of initial education and training will respond more positively to additional training. Accordingly, the experience of past training (*PT*) and education (*E*) is expected to be positively related to current training. Age (*A*) is expected to have a negative effect, partly because of cultural factors (older persons do not view additional education as appropriate) and partly because of economic factors (the returns are uncertain and will be spread over a relatively short period). The region variable (*R*) reflects differences in the availability of jobs and training.

There are expected to be fewer opportunities in Northern and Southern regions than in the rest of the country. Workers in these regions may therefore place a higher value on additional training. But the final outcome should also depend on the relative availability of training opportunities. The same argument applies for the urban/rural variable (*U/R*). The public/private establishment variable (PPE) reflects the differential in training opportunities. Level of skill (*LS*) is similar to education and indicates the likely effect of the accumulated stock of human capital on the returns from investment in additional training. This effect is expected to be negative. The better-off the worker the less likely additional training will be perceived as worthwhile. Accordingly, income adequacy (*IA*) and monthly salary (*MS*) are expected to be negatively related to current training.

Model Specification

The following model is specified for current training (*CT*):

$$CT = CT(E, A, R, U/R, PPE, PT, LS, IA, LC, MS)$$

where   *E* = education, with one of the following values:

>   0, no schooling
>   1, elementary school
>   2, intermediate school
>   3, secondary school
>   4, university or college
>   5, postgraduate

A = age, with one of the following values:

>   0, if under 20 years old
>   1, if 20–24 years old
>   2, if 25–29 years old
>   3, if 30–34 years old
>   4, if 35–39 years old
>   5, if 40–44 years old
>   6, if 45–49 years old
>   7, if 50–54 years old
>   8, if 55–59 years old
>   9, if 60 years or older

R = region, a dummy variable that takes the value of one if in Central, Eastern, or Western region and zero otherwise.

U/R = urban/rural; urban takes the value of one, rural is zero.

PPE = public or private establishment, a dummy variable that takes the value of one if work is in a private establishment and zero otherwise.

PT = past training, a dummy variable, with the value of one if the individual is taking training and zero otherwise.

LS = level of skill, a dummy variable that takes the value of one for higher skills (professional, technical, administrative, managerial, clerical, sales, and services workers) and zero otherwise.

IA = income adequacy, with one of the following values:

>   1, far too little income
>   2, not quite adequate
>   3, adequate
>   4, more than adequate
>   5, much more than adequate

LC = length of current contract, with one of the following values:

>   0, if no contract
>   2, if two-year contract

3, if three-year contract

4, if four-year term or longer term

MS = monthly salary, with one of the following values:

1, less than SR1,000

2, SR1,000–1,499

3, SR1,500–1,999

4, SR2,000–2,999

5, SR3,000–4,999

6, SR5,000–7,499

7, SR7,500 or higher

The analysis is done separately for the 978 workers in the establishment sample and the 756 workers in the household sample. The household sample is more representative of the employment structure of Saudis in the labor force since, unlike the establishment sample, its frame is based on a probability sample of households and not on a census of establishments; that is, it is not confined to the formal sector of employment. Because of the nature of the dependent variable (a dummy variable) and the expected nonlinearity of the relations, a probit model was used (the probit technique is described in the appendix to chapter 8).

The Results

The results of the multivariate analysis for current training are presented in table 6-3. Findings for both the establishment and household samples are specified by a probit estimate, with a *t*-statistic in parentheses. A *t*-value of 1.960 or more indicates significance at 0.05 or better. At the bottom of each column of the table the number of cases, the mean, and the χ^2 statistics (twice log likelihood) are provided.

In the case of the establishment workers, four variables are found to be significant: education, past training, level of skill, and income adequacy. Education and past training are positively related to current training. It seems that the efficiency of assimilating additional training is greater with higher levels of education, and especially when workers have had some previous training. The higher the skill level, however, the lower the perceived value of training. For the establishment sample, the most significant factor concerning current training is income adequacy, which indicates that increased income relative to perceived needs reduces workers' participation in training activities.

The results of the household sample yield some differences from those of the establishment case. There were five significant variables: age, region, urban/rural, past training, and income adequacy. Positively re-

Table 6-3. *Current Training of Saudi Establishment and Household Workers: Multivariate Analysis*
(probit estimates)

Variables	Establishment sample	Household sample
Intercept	−0.685	−0.490
	(−1.128)	(−0.300)
Education	0.186	−0.033
	(2.312)	(−0.481)
Age	−0.065	−0.234
	(−1.610)	(−5.173)
Region	−0.247	−0.360
	(−1.200)	(−2.160)
Urban/rural	—	0.446
		(2.635)
Public/private	−0.460	—
	(−0.460)	
Past training	0.522	0.889
	(2.942)	(5.207)
Level of skill	−0.591	0.308
	(−3.393)	(1.666)
Income adequacy	−0.324	−0.206
	(−5.072)	(−3.287)
Length of current contract	−0.047	0.010
	(−0.410)	(0.055)
Monthly salary	−0.042	−0.092
	(−0.664)	(−1.507)
Number of observations	978	756
Mean dependent variable	0.34	0.22
Degrees of freedom	9	9
χ^2	21.80	79.05

Note: *t*-statistics in parentheses.

lated factors include past training and urban/rural, while age, region, and income adequacy were all negatively related to current training. Past training and age had the expected effect and were the two most significant variables in the household sample.

In general, it seems that it is not easy to provide training to older workers, that more incentives and more training facilities are needed in rural areas, that training is a cumulative process—those who have it once are more likely to obtain additional training when the need arises—and that as their income is perceived as being more adequate, Saudis will be less likely to participate in training activities regardless of their level of skill and productivity.

In the Long Run

To advance long-term skill formation, the Saudi government has placed particular emphasis on the development of specialized skills and high-level manpower. A two-pronged thrust in the development plans called for expenditures on both human resources (education and vocational and technical training) and social development (health care, family care, and child and youth care). As the data in chapter 3 indicated, the results of this emphasis were no less than spectacular. How did the survey's snapshot in time reflect this effort?

Children in School

About one-third of the Saudi workers in the sample did not have children. For the remaining two-thirds, many of their children were relatively young. About half the respondents in both samples had at least one child under school age (less than five years old). Details are found in table 6-4.

How many of the Saudi parents had children in school? As indicated in tables 6-5 and 6-6, 36 percent of the respondents in public establishments and 34 percent of the respondents in private establishments had at least one son in school in Saudi Arabia. The education of girls also seemed to be widespread. About one out of every four respondents reported having at least one daughter in school. A small but significant proportion (between 5 and 13 percent) reported having at least one son in school outside Saudi Arabia. Very few reported the same for daughters.

Table 6-4. *Age of Youngest Son or Daughter for Saudi Respondents* (percent)

| Age of youngest | Establishments | | | | Households | |
| | Public | | Private | | | |
	Sons	Daughters	Sons	Daughters	Sons	Daughters
5	50	65	47	56	53	57
5–9	29	26	25	25	23	26
10–14	11	4	19	9	11	16
15+	10	5	9	10	13	11
Total	100	100	100	100	100	100

As table 6-7 illustrates, there were apparent regional differences in the distribution of households by school attendance. The Northern and Southern regions had fewer households with at least one of their children in school. For adequate comparison, however, these proportions must be standardized for marital status and family size.

Expectations for Children's Education

The expectations of parents for the education of their children reflect in part their aspirations and commitment to invest in the children's future. They also reflect the parents' own valuation of the anticipated benefits from the children's education. The findings for Saudi respondents in the household sample, summarized in table 6-8, show that almost 90 percent

Table 6-5. *Number of Sons and Daughters in School in Saudi Arabia for Respondents in the Establishment Sample*
(percent)

| Number of children | Establishment | | | |
| | Public | | Private | |
	Sons	Daughters	Sons	Daughters
0	64	71	66	76
1–2	19	24	23	12
3–4	15	5	10	7
5+	2	—[a]	1	5
Total	100	100	100	100

a. Less than 0.5 percent.

Table 6-6. *Number of Sons and Daughters in Schools Outside Saudi Arabia for Saudi Respondents in the Establishment Sample*
(percent)

| Number of children | Establishment | | | |
| | Public | | Private | |
	Sons	Daughters	Sons	Daughters
0	95	99	87	97
1+	5	1	13	3
Total	100	100	100	100

Table 6-7. *Saudi Respondents in the Household Sample with at Least One Child in School*
(percent)

| | Educational level | | | | | |
| | Primary | | Secondary | | College | |
Region	Son	Daughter	Son	Daughter	Son	Daughter
Central	50	37	48	29	11	6
Eastern	52	19	30	22	9	4
Northern	36	27	19	10	4	2
Southern	41	21	20	6	4	1
Western	29	36	28	24	6	4
All regions	39	31	34	23	7	4

Table 6-8. *Expectations of Saudi Respondents in the Household Sample of Their Children's Educational Level*
(percent)

| | Less than secondary | | Secondary | | College | | Postgraduate | |
Region	Son	Daughter	Son	Daughter	Son	Daughter	Son	Daughter
Central	—[a]	5	6	11	51	51	40	29
Eastern	2	3	9	22	73	61	14	11
Northern	4	58	13	17	76	16	4	4
Southern	0	17	11	33	86	48	3	1
Western	2	4	4	14	87	81	5	1
All regions	3	8	7	16	73	62	17	12

a. Less than 0.5 percent.

expected their sons to complete at least a college-level degree, and about 74 percent expected the same for their daughters.

There were wide regional variations in the expectations for children's education. Expectations beyond a college degree were highest for both sons and daughters in the Central region (40 and 29 percent, respectively). The largest regional differences were related to expectations about daughters' education. The Northern region had the lowest expectations for daughters' education (only 20 percent envisioned a college education for their girls); the Central and Western regions had the highest (80 to 82 percent, respectively, wanted postsecondary schooling for daughters).

Conclusions

Whether training in the short run or education in the long run, there is evidence of skill formation among Saudi respondents in both the establishment sample and the household sample. The trend of skill formation in Saudi Arabia over time should continue for the foreseeable future. This is a positive development in view of the continuously increasing complexity of new technologies which are being introduced at various levels of the Saudi economy. Of particular significance is the widespread interest in female education. The benefits of female education extend beyond the potential participation of females in the labor market; they have direct implications for the well-being of the next generation. Since skill formation is a time-consuming process, the future skill composition of the labor force is determined by past and present government policies in education, training, and the eradication of illiteracy.

7. Wage and Family Income

THIS CHAPTER FOCUSES on the process of wage and income determination among Saudi respondents only, with some comparison with non-Saudi respondents. Its purpose is to identify the variables which determine wage and income levels and to quantify their relative weight in such a process. The chapter is divided into two sections: the first presents profiles of wages and of family incomes from the establishment and household surveys; the second examines the factors underlying the distribution of labor earnings. The first section may be regarded as a background to the multivariate analysis of the determination of income and wages that follows in the second half of the chapter. The context of the discussion is expressly policy oriented.

Profile of Family Income and Wage Rates

The findings presented here indicate generally higher family income among the Saudi respondents in private establishments than among those in public establishments or households. (The non-Saudi private establishment respondents, however, showed an opposite pattern.) Significant regional differences also emerged. Wage distribution patterns tend to follow those for family income.

Family Income

For the purposes of the present study, family income is defined as the sum of the wages of all of the earners in a family, job benefits (for example, allowances for housing, transportation, child support, and so on), returns on investments, income from rents, transfer payments, and other business income within one year. Frequency distributions of family incomes thus defined are summarized in deciles for the establishment sample (1,055 correspondents) and the household sample (883 respondents) in table 7-1. Differences in decile mean and median incomes between the two samples must be interpreted with caution because no

Table 7-1. *Distribution of Total Family Annual Income:*
Saudi Respondents
(thousands of riyals)

Decile	Establishment sample			Household sample		
	Mean income	Median income	Percentage of total	Mean income	Median income	Percentage of total
First	7.3	8.3	1.5	0.1	0.0[a]	0.0[a]
Second	16.1	16.2	3.3	8.6	9.5	2.1
Third	21.3	21.3	4.3	14.7	14.4	3.7
Fourth	25.8	25.5	5.3	21.1	21.6	5.3
Fifth	30.8	30.6	6.3	26.6	26.4	6.6
Sixth	36.3	36.1	7.4	33.6	34.4	8.3
Seventh	44.3	43.4	9.0	42.1	42.0	10.5
Eighth	57.2	57.7	11.6	52.0	51.6	12.9
Ninth	81.4	80.0	16.6	65.4	64.1	16.2
Tenth	178.8	149.9	34.7	134.2	99.3	34.4
Total	49.3	33.1	100.0	40.1	29.8	100.0

a. Less than 0.05.

attempt has been made to control for family composition—for example, the number of wage earners or the number of dependents.

From table 7-1 it is possible to construct Lorenz curves for Saudi establishment and household respondents (see figure 7-1). The two distributions are remarkably similar. In fact, they coincide for the ninth and tenth deciles. They differ, however, in the first six deciles, where family income is distributed less equitably among the household sample. Differentials between mean and median incomes measure the degree of skewness in income distribution, whether within the same sample for each decile or across the two samples.

Within each decile the differences between mean and median incomes are not significant, except in the tenth decile. It thus appears that the significant mean-median differentials for the samples as a whole are the direct results of those differentials only in the tenth decile. When the two samples are compared, the mean and median values for all deciles are uniformly higher in the establishment sample: SR49,300 and SR33,100 respectively, compared with SR40,100 and SR29,800 in the household sample. The ratio of median to mean incomes is higher in the household sample, however, indicating greater skewness in the distribution of family incomes.

A comparison of the distribution of family incomes in the five regions suggests substantial regional variations. Among Saudi public establish-

Figure 7-1. *The Lorenz Curve for Saudi Respondents: Establishment and Household Samples*

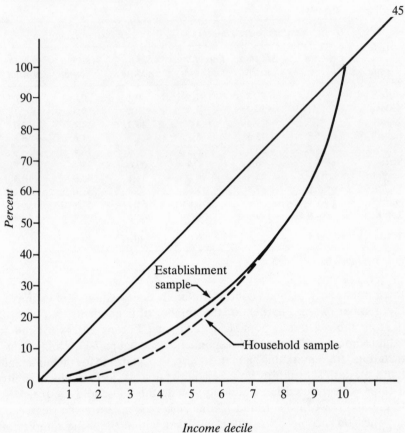

Income decile

ment workers, the highest-income families lived in the Eastern and Western regions (where the respective median total family incomes were SR51,000 and SR43,200) while the lowest-income families lived in the Southern region (median = SR31,200). The pattern is different for non-Saudi establishment workers and for both Saudi and non-Saudi households. Among non-Saudi public establishment workers the highest-income families were in the Eastern and Southern regions (respective medians both SR43,000), and the lowest-income families were in the Northern region (median = SR24,200). Among Saudi and non-Saudi households the richest families were in the Central (Saudi median = SR44,000; non-Saudi median = SR43,700) and Western (Saudi median

= SR51,200; non-Saudi median = SR42,700) regions, while the poorest were in the Southern region (Saudi median = SR24,900; non-Saudi median = SR23,400).

Wages

Data on the statistical means of current wages are summarized below (large establishments are those with at least twenty employees; small are those with less than twenty):

		Establishment sample			
			Private		*Household*
Nationality	*Public*	*All*	*Large*	*Small*	*sample*
Saudis	34.4	34.7	24.8	42.6	33.2
Non-Saudis	31.0	22.1	23.5	21.0	32.1

These wage figures present a pattern similar to that reported in table 7-1 for total income. Among Saudis the estimated median annual wage was more than SR33,000 for both samples taken as a whole. Saudi private establishment workers as a group earned a slightly higher wage than either household respondents or workers in public establishments. Many of those higher-paid workers, however, were employed in small establishments. In fact, workers in large private establishments received on the average the lowest wages (median = SR24,800) paid to Saudis.

Non-Saudis on the average received lower wages than their Saudi counterparts, although the differences were not very substantial in the public or household samples. Among non-Saudis those in public establishments made more on the average than workers in private establishments. This was especially true when public establishment workers were compared with workers in small private establishments: the difference between the median annual wages of these two groups was SR10,000.

A comparison of median annual wages in the five regions indicates no clear pattern. Among Saudi respondents in all but the large private establishments, however, those in the Southern region generally received the lowest wages. Thus the median public establishment annual wage for Saudis in the Southern region was SR23,600 compared with a SR34,400 median for all regions. In small private establishments, however, the Saudi median in the South was SR13,800 (all regions = SR42,600); in the Saudi household sample the Southern region emerged with a median of SR23,000 (all regions = SR33,200). For non-Saudis there was no discernible regional pattern. Thus regional location had no uniform effect on the overall difference between Saudi and non-Saudi wages.

With this background information on the differences and similarities in patterns of wages and family income nationally and regionally, we can now focus on the determinants of wage differentials among Saudi workers, which will be analyzed by controlling for occupation, education, and age, among other factors.

Determinants of Wage Rates and Family Income

The labor market in Saudi Arabia has undergone significant structural changes. As a result, several questions have arisen: What are the implications of such changes for the determination of labor earnings? Does labor income vary with basic socioeconomic characteristics in a way predictable from the interplay of market forces? Is there a positive relation between the level of wages and the accumulation of human capital, that is, education and training? Do earnings have the expected pattern over the various stages of the life cycle? These are important questions to be addressed during the process of formulating policy and planning.

To answer some of these questions, one needs to construct a model. In the present analysis it is difficult to rely on any given theoretical framework for three reasons: first, past knowledge about the Saudi labor market is rudimentary; second, the market itself is constantly undergoing structural changes; third, the current study is essentially without precedent in the Saudi context, which makes it difficult to evaluate the validity of the measured concepts. Accordingly, the present analysis should be viewed as exploratory. The choice of the explanatory variables is pragmatic, since it is based on theoretical considerations combined with policy relevance.

The starting point for the analysis is the examination of the bivariate relation between labor earnings per month (salary) or per year (family income) and each of the three central variables: age, education, and occupation. In the case of age and labor earnings in the establishment sample, median monthly salary reached a peak at age 40–49 and declined thereafter. It increased monotonically from SR1,470 at age 20 or younger to SR4,400 at age 40–49 and dropped to SR2,240 for those 50 or older (see figure 7-2). This nonlinear pattern also held for family income. In the latter case, however, the peak was reached at an earlier age (30–39). The same general pattern held for the household sample.

The bivariate relation between education and monthly salary showed median monthly salary increasing monotonically with the level of education. For the establishment sample, median monthly salary increased by

Figure 7-2. *Saudi Labor Earnings by Age: Gross Bivariate Relationship*

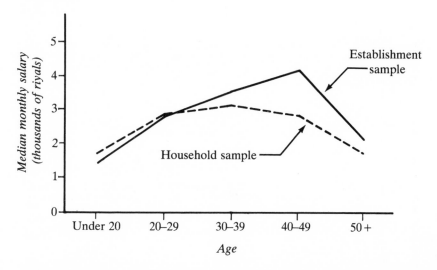

about 50 percent between those without formal education (median = SR2,270) and those with secondary education (median = SR3,400). The largest difference in monthly salary was between those with secondary education and those with college degrees—having a college degree more than doubled monthly salary (figure 7-3). This positive relationship between education and monthly salary held true for the household sample. The relation between education and family income had essentially the same general pattern.

At this point an examination of the combined effects of age and education on monthly salary is revealing. Figure 7-4, based on unweighted data, shows estimates of median monthly salary by age and by education for the establishment sample. A generally similar profile emerges for the household sample. These findings can be viewed as separate age-earnings profiles for different levels of education. In the first place, and as discussed below, earnings increased by education at a given age. In the second place, the effect of age on earnings depended on the level of education; that is, at higher levels of education earnings increased by age systematically. However, the number of relevant observations decreased significantly for older people with higher education. The implications of these findings for the effect of government investment in education on income distribution are self-evident. There is strong evi-

Figure 7-3. *Saudi Labor Earnings by Education: Gross Bivariate Relationship*

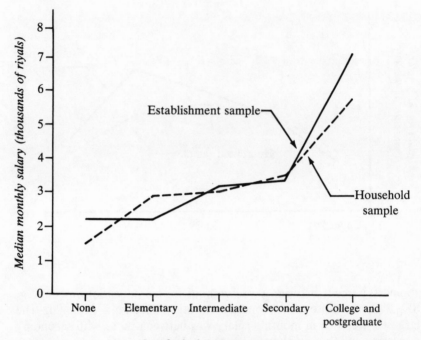

Level of education completed

dence that education is positively related to earnings, and this will be confirmed by the more in-depth analysis to be carried out in the following section with the use of multivariate techniques.

With the bivariate relationship between occupation and earnings for the establishment sample (see figure 7-5), the highest median salary income was reported for the managerial and administrative professions (SR7,850) followed by the professionals (SR4,070). The lowest median monthly salary was for service workers (SR1,550). The same general pattern prevailed for family income and for the household sample.

The relationships between labor earnings on the one hand and age, education, and occupation on the other were all in the expected direction, but they have to be interpreted with care. What is being observed is a pattern of the gross (unadjusted) relationship, which includes the effects of other variables. Part of the apparent effects of education, for example, may be due to differences in the educational levels and age structure of workers in the various occupational categories. Managers

Figure 7-4. *Monthly Salary by Age and Education: Saudi Establishment Sample*

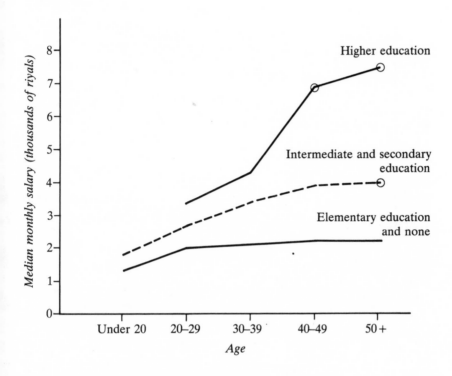

Note: Circled points indicate less than twenty cases.

and professionals are relatively more educated and tend to reach their positions at a relatively older age—a pattern that is further complicated to the extent that higher education is more prevalent among the younger generation of Saudis. For these reasons, only multivariate analysis can capture the complex structure underlying income and wage determination and thus estimate the partial contribution of the explanatory variables.

Model Specification

Labor earnings are represented by two dependent variables: monthly salary and family income. In this study the main focus is on monthly

Figure 7-5. *Saudi Labor Earnings by Occupation: Gross Bivariate Relationship*

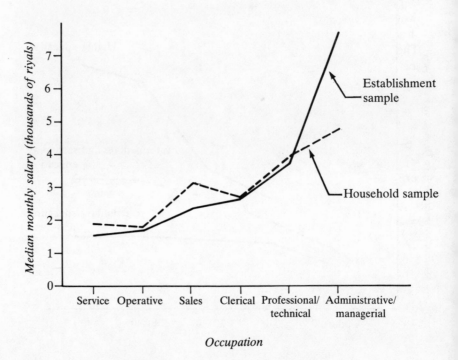

Occupation

salary and its determination in the labor market. Monthly salary (for the respondents' current main job) was obtained as a direct measure of amounts paid by employers in Saudi riyals. Although they do not include fringe benefits, they are a good approximation of job remuneration. Family income was obtained by adding annual income reported from all sources. It represents the current economic position of the respondent. The findings on family income should supplement those of monthly salary.

Two groups of variables are used as explanatory factors: the first comprises ability and skills; the second, differentials in opportunities. Formal education and past training represent differences in ability and skills. The quality and quantity of jobs available represent opportunity differentials according to the region of current residence and whether the respondent works in a public or private establishment. Finally, age, which is partly a measure of experience and partly a measure of seniority, and occupation, which is a combination of the measure of the level of skill and responsibility, represent a mixture of those two groups. Note, however, that occupational classification does not necessarily correspond with a unique skill classification.

The following five models are specified, two for monthly salary and three for family income:

$$MSE = MSE \ (R, PPE, O, A, E, PT) \quad (7.1)$$
$$MSH = MSH \ (R, O, A, E, PT) \quad (7.2)$$
$$FIE = FIE \ (R, PPE, O, A, E, PT) \quad (7.3)$$
$$FIH = FIH \ (R, EM, A, E, PT) \quad (7.4)$$
$$FIH^* = FIH^* \ (R, O, A, E, PT) \quad (7.5)$$

where MSE = monthly salary of workers in the establishment sample and is coded as follows:

> 1, less than SR1,000
> 2, SR1,000–SR1,499
> 3, SR1,500–SR1,999
> 4, SR2,000–SR2,999
> 5, SR3,000–SR4,999
> 6, SR5,000–SR7,499
> 7, SR7,500 or higher

MSH = monthly salary of those respondents in the household sample who are working for an employer and is coded similarly to MSE above.

FIE = family income of workers in the establishment sample and is coded as follows:

> 1, less than SR5,000 per year
> 2, SR5,000–SR14,999 per year
> 3, SR15,000–SR24,999 per year
> 4, SR25,000–SR34,999 per year
> 5, SR35,000–SR44,999 per year
> 6, SR45,000–SR54,999 per year
> 7, SR55,000 or higher per year

FIH = family income of all respondents in the household sample and is coded similarly to FIE above.

FIH^* = family income of those respondents in the household sample who are working for an employer and is coded similarly to FIE above.

Detailed classifications of the following explanatory variables are specified in tables 7-4 to 7-30 in appendix A to this chapter:

R = region (tables 7-8, 7-14, 7-18, 7-24, 7-29)
PPE = public/private establishment (tables 7-9, 7-20)
O = current occupation (tables 7-6, 7-12, 7-17, 7-28)
A = age (tables 7-5, 7-11, 7-16, 7-22, 7-27)
E = education (tables 7-4, 7-10, 7-15, 7-21, 7-26)
PT = past training (tables 7-7, 7-13, 7-19, 7-25, 7-30)
EM = employment status (table 7-23)

Models (7.1) and (7.2) for the establishment and household samples, respectively, indicate that the level of monthly salary is a function of region, occupation, age, education, and past training. For the establishment sample, a variable indicating whether the respondent is working for a public or private establishment (PPE) is included. This variable is not applicable in the household sample in which wages are estimated only for respondents who are not self-employed but working for someone else. Accordingly, the analysis for model (7.2) is restricted to this group. Models (7.3)–(7.5) for family income have essentially the same specification. Equation (7.4), however, includes all household respondents, while equation (7.5), like equation (7.2), is restricted to those working for an employer.

Estimation Technique

To estimate the specified models, multiple classification analysis (MCA) as detailed in appendix B to this chapter is used. This is essentially a multiple dummy variable regression with some advantages over conventional dummy variable regressions.

Results for Monthly Salary

The results of the multivariate analysis for monthly salary are summarized in table 7-2.[1] As the table indicates, on the basis of the beta ranking, education is the most important factor explaining differences in monthly salary, followed by age and occupation, and there is a close similarity between the findings for the establishment sample and the household sample. Age and education are the two most important variables in both cases. The role of previous training is relatively more important in the household sample. It replaces occupation following age and education. The beta coefficient for region is almost identical for both samples (0.13).

Table 7-2. *Characteristics of Respondents Used to Explain Monthly Salary for Saudi Workers: Multiple Classification Analysis*

| | Relative importance (beta coefficient) | |
| | Establishment sample | Household sample |
Characteristic		
Education	0.440	0.520
Age	0.347	0.261
Occupation	0.245	0.119
Public or private establishment	0.157	—
Region	0.127	0.126
Previous training	0.103	0.250
Number of cases (N)	1,016	523
Y	1,960	1,832
SD_y	338	461
$\bar{R}^2$	0.408	0.427

Note: Both mean (Y) and standard deviation (SD_y) are stated in terms of Saudi riyals (SR).

The $\bar{R}^2$ is relatively large in both cases (0.41 and 0.43 for the establishment and household sample, respectively).

The detailed effects of the various explanatory factors are given in the tables in appendix A to this chapter. A summary of the "pure" effects of education, age, and occupation is given in figures 7-6 to 7-8. As figure 7-6 indicates, the level of education clearly affects monthly salary. Having a college degree almost doubles the monthly salary earned with no education at all. Even after adjusting for the effect of other relevant variables, the effect of education remains strong and in the expected direction. Thus, government expenditures on education in Saudi Arabia have significant positive effects on labor earnings, as reflected in the wage differentials for various levels of education.

The results of the MCA for the "pure" effect of age on monthly salary are equally revealing (figure 7-7). A person's wage rate was found to rise between the ages of 30 and 45, presumably because of increased experience and skills. After 45 or 50, the wage rate may decline, probably because of decreased dexterity, flexibility, stamina, or even reluctance to change jobs for fear of losing seniority or pension. Age differences in a cross-section do not, of course, reflect what happens to an individual over time. As figure 7-7 indicates, wages increase by age up to about 40–50

Figure 7-6. *Multiple Classification Analysis for Monthly Salary: The Effect of Education*

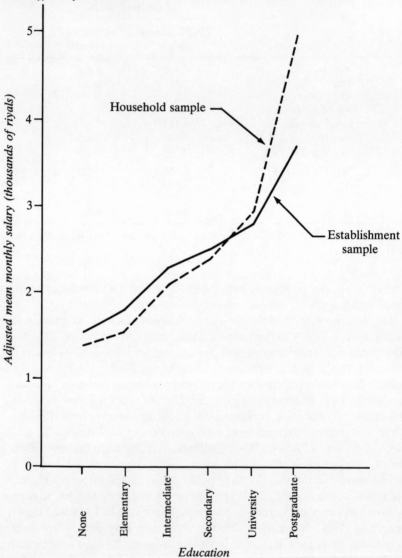

Note: Mean monthly salary is adjusted for the effect of other explanatory variables included in the model (table 7-2).

years of age when it levels off and declines at older ages. Tables 7-5 and
7-11 show that the adjusted means differ markedly from the unadjusted
ones. These differences arise because the unadjusted means include the
effects of other variables such as occupation and education. When these
are accounted for, the effect of age becomes smoother, reflecting to some
extent the role of seniority in wage determination.

The "pure" effect of occupation on the average monthly salary is that
salary is highest among administrators, managers, and professionals, and
lowest for service workers (tables 7-6, 7-12, figure 7-8). Although these
findings are similar to those reported earlier under gross bivariate analy-

Figure 7-7. *Multiple Classification Analysis for Monthly Salary:
The Effect of Age*

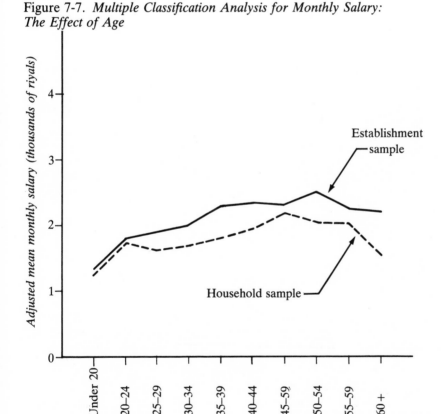

Note: Mean monthly salary is adjusted for the effect of other explanatory variables
included in the model (table 7-2).

sis (GBA) for the extreme points of the occupational distribution (figure 7-5), they are significantly different for the distribution as a whole. Under the GBA, the salary differentials among occupations are very pronounced and thus statistically significant. Under MCA, however, such differentials are much less pronounced and thus not statistically significant, especially in the household sample (see table 7-3). More important, except for the

Figure 7-8. *Multiple Classification Analysis for Monthly Salary: The Effect of Occupation*

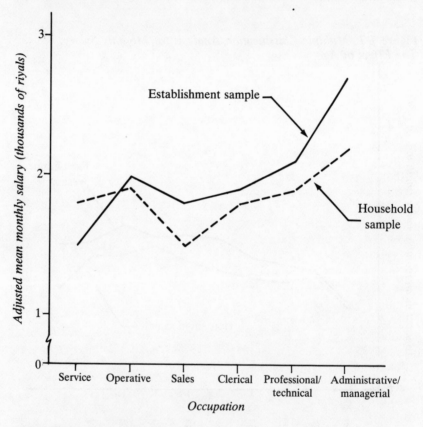

Note: Mean monthly salary is adjusted for the effect of other explanatory variables included in the model (table 7-2).

Table 7-3. *Monthly Salary for Saudi Respondents
under Alternative Methods of Analysis*
(thousands of riyals)

Occupation	Gross bivariate analysis		Multiple classification analysis	
	Estab-lish-ment sample	House-hold sample	Estab-lish-ment sample	House-hold sample
Service	1.5	1.9	1.5	1.8
Operative	1.7	1.8	2.0	1.9
Sales	2.3	3.2	1.8	1.5
Clerical	2.6	2.7	1.9	1.8
Professional/technical	3.8	4.0	2.1	1.9
Administrative/managerial	7.7	4.8	2.7	2.2

services and operative labor categories, mean salaries adjusted under MCA are uniformly well *below* median salaries under GBA, although for the country as a whole unadjusted mean salaries are significantly above median salaries. One possible explanation for this reduced difference is that there may be discrimination on the basis of age or education in the recruitment of workers. As a result, the effect of occupation is reduced when accounting for age and education.

Other important findings pertain to the effect of past training, region, and type of employing enterprise. It is evident that past training has a significant effect (tables 7-7, 7-13). Expenditures on job training seem to be socially justified, judging by the positive effects of training on labor earnings independent of and supplemental to formal education. The findings which relate to the effect of regions show regional variations in monthly salary. On the average, wages are highest in the East and lowest in the North even after adjustment for all other characteristics (tables 7-8, 7-14). A possible explanation is that the Eastern region is relatively more industrialized, with possibly the highest demand for skilled Saudis. The Northern region, by contrast, is the least industrialized and is where the demand for skilled Saudis tends to be low. For the establishment sample, monthly salary is higher (by about 12 percent or more) in private than in public enterprises. Thus, after wage differences are adjusted for education, age, occupation, past training, and region, significant differences still persist between public and private enterprises. One possible explanation is that the private sector lacks the strict salary ranges and promotion codes of the public sector.

Results for Family Income

The results of the models for family income are shown in tables 7-15 to 7-30. On the basis of the beta ranking, education is the most important factor explaining differences in annual family income, followed by age. This pattern is the same for both samples. A comparison with the preceding findings on monthly salary indicates close similarities to the findings on family income. As is the case with monthly salary, for example, past training is relatively more important in the household than in the establishment sample. The similarities are not surprising since salary income is a significant component of family income.[2]

Conclusions

The results of this chapter, whether derived from the establishment sample or the household sample, unmistakably show the central role of education and training in determining wage rates and family incomes. Thus, government investment in education and training shows substantial positive effects on the earnings of Saudi labor. Age in traditional societies usually indicates experience and is therefore the main factor in wage determination. In Saudi Arabia, by contrast, although large-scale modernization is only a recent phenomenon, the effects of education and skill formation are more important than age. In other words, the influence of modernization is stronger than the influence of tradition in determining wage rates in the Saudi labor market.

Wage differentials by occupation contain the effects of age and education, but after adjusting for these factors, wage differentials by occupation continue to exist. Job responsibilities and characteristics may partly explain the adjusted wage differentials, but only partly. The pressures of demand on certain occupations—for example, operative labor—provide another partial explanation.

By comparison with the other explanatory factors, the region variable, although statistically significant, has a weak effect. Interregionally, therefore, there are no inherent wage differentials.

After considering the workers' education-occupation-age mix, money wage rates are higher in private than in public enterprises because of the higher rate of educational experience and skills. Such differentials in money wages are counterbalanced by nonmonetary considerations in the public sector, such as security and prestige. Nevertheless, there are inherent dangers of brain drain from government to the private sector if present wage differentials continue in the future. For this reason it appears appropriate for the government to explore alternative methods and programs to ensure its ability to compete in the labor market, especially for qualified workers.

Appendix A. Detailed Classification of Explanatory Variables

Tables 7-4 to 7-30, which follow, offer detailed classifications of the following explanatory variables as discussed in the preceding text:

R = region (tables 7-8, 7-14, 7-18, 7-24, 7-29)
PPE = public/private establishment (tables 7-9, 7-20)
O = current occupation (tables 7-6, 7-12, 7-17, 7-28)
A = age (tables 7-5, 7-11, 7-16, 7-22, 7-27)
E = education (tables 7-4, 7-10, 7-15, 7-21, 7-26)
PT = past training (tables 7-7, 7-13, 7-19, 7-25, 7-30)
EM = employment status (table 7-23)

The source of all tables in this appendix is an analysis of the labor market study computer tape.

Table 7-4. *The Effect of Education on Monthly Salary: Saudi Workers Sample, 1978*

Education	Number of observations	Unadjusted mean (code)	Adjusted mean	
			Code	Thousands of riyals
None	245	3.19	3.15	1.58
Elementary	321	3.65	3.66	1.83
Intermediate	197	4.28	4.38	2.38
Secondary	163	4.45	4.50	2.50
University	80	5.08	4.84	2.84
Postgraduate	10	5.60	5.36	3.73

Table 7-5. *The Effect of Age on Monthly Salary: Saudi Workers Sample, 1978*

Age	Number of obser- vations	Unadjusted mean (code)	Adjusted mean	
			Code	Thousands of riyals
Under 20	79	2.57	2.77	1.39
20–24	208	3.76	3.53	1.77
25–29	179	4.16	3.80	1.90
30–34	133	4.26	4.03	2.03
35–39	112	4.26	4.31	2.31
40–44	123	4.03	4.38	2.38
45–49	94	3.93	4.34	2.34
50–54	47	4.04	4.48	2.48
55–59	18	4.06	4.30	2.30
60+	23	3.70	4.23	2.23

Table 7-6. *The Effect of Occupation on Monthly Salary: Saudi Workers Sample, 1978*

Occupation	Number of obser- vations	Unadjusted mean (code)	Adjusted mean	
			Code	Thousands of riyals
Professional/technical	55	4.73	4.10	2.10
Administrative/managerial	79	5.35	4.72	2.72
Clerical	422	3.79	3.89	1.95
Sales	70	3.99	3.68	1.84
Service	63	2.41	3.02	1.51
Operative and other	327	3.65	3.96	1.98

Table 7-7. *The Effect of Previous Training on Monthly Salary: Saudi Workers Sample, 1978*

Previous training	Number of obser- vations	Unadjusted mean (code)	Adjusted mean	
			Code	Thousands of riyals
No	849	3.78	3.86	1.69
Yes	167	4.62	4.23	2.23

Table 7-8. *The Effect of Region on Monthly Salary:*
Saudi Workers Sample, 1978

Region	Number of observations	Unadjusted mean (code)	Adjusted mean	
			Code	Thousands of riyals
Central	284	3.87	3.88	1.94
Eastern	307	4.17	4.17	2.17
Northern	54	3.46	3.75	1.88
Southern	58	3.69	3.91	1.95
Western	313	3.85	3.75	1.88

Table 7-9. *The Effect of Establishment on Monthly Salary:*
Saudi Workers Sample, 1978

Type of Establishment	Number of observations	Unadjusted mean (code)	Adjusted mean	
			Code	Thousands of riyals
Public	244	3.85	3.55	1.78
Private, small	45	3.98	4.23	2.23
Private, large	727	3.94	4.03	2.03

Table 7-10. *The Effect of Level of Education on Monthly Salary:*
Total Saudi Household Sample, 1978

Education	Number of observations	Unadjusted mean (code)	Adjusted mean	
			Code	Thousands of riyals
None	176	2.76	2.76	1.38
Elementary	142	3.51	3.61	1.53
Intermediate	90	4.30	4.22	2.11
Secondary	63	4.48	4.41	2.41
University	50	5.02	4.96	2.96
Postgraduate	2	6.50	5.98	4.95

Table 7-11. *The Effect of Age on Monthly Salary:*
Total Saudi Household Sample, 1978

			Adjusted mean	
Age	Number of observations	Unadjusted mean (code)	Code	Thousands of riyals
Under 20	9	2.56	2.57	1.28
20–24	51	4.00	3.50	1.75
25–29	82	3.73	3.27	1.65
30–34	72	3.82	3.32	1.66
35–39	83	3.94	3.70	1.85
40–44	69	3.59	3.93	1.97
45–49	67	3.84	4.24	2.24
50–54	42	3.33	4.05	2.05
55–59	26	3.35	4.03	2.03
60+	22	2.23	3.18	1.59

Table 7-12. *The Effect of Occupation on Monthly Salary:*
Total Saudi Household Sample, 1978

			Adjusted mean	
Occupation	Number of observations	Unadjusted mean (code)	Code	Thousands of riyals
Professional/technical	95	4.59	3.81	1.91
Administrative/managerial	26	5.15	4.17	2.17
Clerical	141	3.57	3.58	1.79
Sales	11	3.36	3.00	1.50
Service	135	3.11	3.58	1.79
Operative and other	115	3.35	3.70	1.85

Table 7-13. *The Effect of Previous Training on Monthly Salary:*
Total Saudi Household Sample, 1978

			Adjusted mean	
Previous training	Number of observations	Unadjusted mean (code)	Code	Thousands of riyals
No	379	3.33	3.44	1.72
Yes	144	4.54	4.26	2.36

Table 7-14. *The Effect of Region on Monthly Salary:*
Total Saudi Household Sample, 1978

Region	Number of obser-vations	Unadjusted mean (code)	Adjusted mean	
			Code	Thousands of riyals
Central	116	3.68	3.55	1.78
Eastern	115	4.17	3.99	1.99
Northern	74	3.18	3.52	1.76
Southern	95	3.30	3.91	1.95
Western	123	3.76	3.68	1.84

Table 7-15. *The Effect of Level of Education on Family Income:*
Saudi Workers Sample, 1978

Education	Number of observations	Unadjusted mean (code)	Adjusted mean	
			Code	Thousands of riyals
None	249	3.70	3.63	2.13
Elementary	322	4.04	4.09	2.59
Intermediate	198	4.65	4.78	3.28
Secondary	170	5.02	5.09	3.59
University	83	5.87	5.54	4.04
Postgraduate	10	6.00	5.67	4.17

Table 7-16. *The Effect of Age on Family Income:*
Saudi Workers Sample, 1978

Age	Number of obser-vations	Unadjusted mean (code)	Adjusted mean	
			Code	Thousands of riyals
Under 20	81	2.96	3.23	1.73
20–24	207	4.03	3.81	2.31
25–29	181	4.61	4.21	2.71
30–34	137	4.68	4.45	2.95
35–39	114	4.91	4.94	3.44
40–44	123	4.40	4.78	3.28
45–49	96	4.70	5.09	3.59
50–54	49	4.80	5.24	3.74
55–59	20	5.00	5.29	3.79
60+	24	4.58	5.13	3.63

Table 7-17. *The Effect of Occupation on Family Income: Saudi Workers Sample, 1978*

Occupation	Number of obser- vations	Unadjusted mean (code)	Adjusted mean	
			Code	Thousands of riyals
Professional/technical	55	5.49	4.80	3.30
Administrative/managerial	85	5.98	5.27	3.77
Clerical	423	4.34	4.31	2.81
Sales	82	5.07	4.66	3.16
Service	62	2.94	3.49	1.99
Operative and other	325	4.01	4.34	2.84

Table 7-18. *The Effect of Region on Family Income: Saudi Workers Sample, 1978*

Region	Number of obser- vations	Unadjusted mean (code)	Adjusted mean	
			Code	Thousands of riyals
Central	279	4.30	4.34	2.84
Eastern	312	4.79	4.81	3.31
Northern	55	4.00	4.17	2.67
Southern	63	4.46	4.56	3.06
Western	323	4.18	4.09	2.59

Table 7-19. *The Effect of Previous Training on Family Income: Saudi Workers Sample, 1978*

Previous training	Number of obser- vations	Unadjusted mean (code)	Adjusted mean	
			Code	Thousands of riyals
No	864	4.24	4.33	2.83
Yes	168	5.27	4.81	3.31

Table 7-20. *The Effect of Establishment on Family Income:*
Saudi Workers Sample, 1978

Type of establishment	Number of observations	Unadjusted mean (code)	Adjusted mean	
			Code	Thousands of riyals
Public	242	4.50	4.16	2.66
Private, small	58	4.97	4.99	3.49
Private, large	732	4.33	4.44	2.94

Table 7-21. *The Effect of Level of Education on Family Income:*
Total Saudi Household Sample, 1978

Education	Number of observations	Unadjusted mean (code)	Adjusted mean	
			Code	Thousands of riyals
None	363	3.80	3.67	2.17
Elementary	200	4.13	4.20	2.70
Intermediate	117	5.17	5.24	3.74
Secondary	92	5.73	5.89	4.39
University	62	6.16	6.31	4.81
Postgraduate	6	7.00	6.71	5.21

Table 7-22. *The Effect of Age on Family Income:*
Total Saudi Household Sample, 1978

Age	Number of observations	Unadjusted mean (code)	Adjusted mean	
			Code	Thousands of riyals
Under 20	22	3.86	3.88	2.38
20–24	71	4.89	4.23	2.73
25–29	105	4.60	3.86	2.36
30–34	92	4.74	4.12	2.62
35–39	112	4.80	4.47	2.97
40–44	108	4.29	4.45	2.85
45–49	106	4.48	4.84	3.34
50–54	82	3.94	4.53	3.03
55–59	66	4.26	4.95	3.45
60 +	76	4.32	5.22	3.72

Table 7-23. *The Effect of Employment Status on Family Income: Total Saudi Household Sample, 1978*

Employment status	Number of observations	Unadjusted mean (code)	Adjusted mean	
			Code	Thousands of riyals
Employed	533	4.62	4.50	3.00
Family business	61	4.34	4.82	3.32
Self-employed	175	4.35	4.64	3.14
Unemployed	4	1.75	2.32	0.82
Retired	26	3.54	3.63	2.13
Sick	4	3.75	3.49	1.99
Never worked or still in school	17	4.77	3.87	2.37
Don't know or other	20	3.80	3.53	2.03

Table 7-24. *The Effect of Region on Family Income: Total Saudi Household Sample, 1978*

Region	Number of observations	Unadjusted mean (code)	Adjusted mean	
			Code	Thousands of riyals
Central	178	4.69	4.53	3.03
Eastern	162	5.04	4.87	3.37
Northern	1,455	3.99	4.25	2.75
Southern	150	3.87	4.08	2.58
Western	205	4.62	4.56	3.06

Table 7-25. *The Effect of Past Training on Family Income: Total Saudi Household Sample, 1978*

Past training	Number of observations	Unadjusted mean (code)	Adjusted mean	
			Code	Thousands of riyals
No	656	4.23	4.35	2.85
Yes	184	5.35	4.94	3.44

Table 7-26. *The Effect of Level of Education on Family Income:*
Reduced Saudi Household Sample, 1978

Education	Number of observations	Unadjusted mean (code)	Adjusted mean	
			Code	Thousands of riyals
None	177	3.64	3.61	2.11
Elementary	145	4.30	4.39	2.89
Intermediate	91	5.28	5.19	3.68
Secondary	65	5.79	5.72	4.22
University	51	6.22	6.22	4.72
Postgraduate	2	7.00	6.54	5.04

Table 7-27. *The Effect of Age on Family Income:*
Reduced Saudi Household Sample, 1978

Age	Number of obser- vations	Unadjusted mean (code)	Adjusted mean	
			Code	Thousands of riyals
Under 20	10	4.30	4.32	2.82
20–24	51	5.00	4.41	2.91
25–29	83	4.60	4.07	2.57
30–34	73	4.66	4.08	2.58
35–39	84	4.96	4.69	3.19
40–44	71	4.37	4.75	3.25
45–49	68	4.60	5.09	3.59
50–54	42	4.02	4.86	3.36
55–59	27	4.82	5.52	4.02
60+	22	4.14	5.26	3.76

Table 7-28. *The Effect of Occupation on Family Income:*
Reduced Saudi Household Sample, 1978

Occupation	Number of observations	Unadjusted mean (code)	Adjusted mean	
			Code	Thousands of riyals
Professional/technical	97	5.74	4.79	3.29
Administrative/managerial	26	6.39	5.21	3.72
Clerical	145	4.61	4.62	3.12
Sales	11	4.00	3.67	2.17
Service	136	3.89	4.50	2.90
Operative and other	116	4.18	4.55	2.95

Table 7-29. *The Effect of Region on Family Income:*
Reduced Saudi Household Sample, 1978

			Adjusted mean	
Region	Number of observations	Unadjusted mean (code)	Code	Thousands of riyals
Central	119	4.69	4.51	3.01
Eastern	117	5.13	4.98	3.48
Northern	76	3.88	4.22	2.72
Southern	95	4.14	4.42	2.92
Western	124	4.87	4.76	3.26

Table 7-30. *The Effect of Previous Training on Family Income:*
Reduced Saudi Household Sample, 1978

			Adjusted mean	
Previous training	Number of observations	Unadjusted mean (code)	Code	Thousands of riyals
No	385	4.52	4.38	2.88
Yes	146	5.51	5.22	3.72

Note: Tables 7-26 through 7-30 report results of model equation (7.5), which limits household respondents to those working for an employer.

Appendix B. Multiple Classification Analysis (MCA)

Most of the predictors specified in the models presented in the text above have nominal measures (for example, education, occupation, region).[3] For the purpose of estimation, a multiple regression using dummy variables is required. To estimate the specified models, multiple classification analysis (MCA) is used. It is essentially a multiple dummy variable regression with some advantages over conventional dummy variable regressions.[4] It provides for a more convenient input arrangement and an understandable output format that focuses on *sets* of predictors, such as education or occupation groups, and on the extent and direction of the adjustments made for intercorrelations among the sets of predictors.[5] Without requiring that the variables be measured on interval scales, that the specified relationships be linear, or the distributions be bivariate normal, the MCA estimates the effect of each predictor on the dependent variable both before and after taking into account the effect of all other variables included in the model. This lack of restrictive assumptions is a great advantage over other traditional methods such as analysis of covariance, multiple regression, or discriminant functions.

The statistical model used by the MCA program takes the following form:[6]

$$Y_{ijk...} = \bar{Y} + a_i + b_j + ... + e_{ijk...}$$

where $Y_{ijk...}$ = the score (on the dependent variable) of individual k who falls in category i of predictor A, category j of predictor B, and so on

$\bar{Y}$ = grand mean of the dependent variable

a_i = the "effect" of membership in the ith category of predictor A

$e_{ijk...}$ = error term of this individual

The adjusted coefficients can be thought of as having been estimated to provide the best possible fit to the observed data by solving the "normal equations" familiar in regression analysis by the use of an iterative procedure. Aside from the adjusted coefficients, the program produces a partial beta coefficient for each predictor (β_i). These betas indicate the relative importance of the various predictors in their joint explanation of the dependent variable. The formula for the calculation of the beta coefficient is:

$$\beta_i = \sqrt{D_i/T}$$

where D_i = sum of squares based on adjusted deviation for predictor i.

T = total sum of squares.

Finally, a coefficient of determination (R^2) adjusted for degrees of freedom is also reported to indicate the percentage of variance explained. Its formula for the MCA program is:

$$R^2 \text{ (adjusted)} = 1 - \left[\frac{(T-E)/(N-C+P-1)}{T/(N-1)} \right]$$

where T = total sum of squares

E = explained sum of squares

N = number of individuals

C = total number of categories across all predictors

P = number of predictors.

Notes

1. The multivariate analysis was done with unweighted data to obtain efficient estimates. Accordingly, percentages and means reported in this section may not be comparable to those reported elsewhere in this book. Strictly speaking, estimates, averages, or distributions reported for multivariate analysis in this report represent the characteristic of the sample population and not of the Saudi Kingdom as a whole. For the latter, the reader should refer to the weighted estimates. However, the estimation of relationships, which is the main focus of the multivariate analysis, is more efficient when unweighted data are used, since the weights reflect differences in intergroup variance. For more details see Leslie Kish, *Survey Sampling* (New York: Wiley, 1965).

2. Assuming a full-time job, with no second job, average annual wage income would be SR23,520 and SR21,984 for the establishment and household samples, respectively (unweighted). These are approximately 80 percent and 70 percent of family income, respectively.

3. For this discussion, scales may be classified into nominal, ordinal, and interval levels of measurement. A nominal scale is one which categorizes objects (such as regions: North, Central, East, South, West). An ordinal scale classifies items and assumes the categories are arranged in some meaningful order (such as educational levels). An interval scale requires classification, ordering, and equal distance between the categories (such as age groups). See, for example, the pioneering discussion by S. S. Stevens, "On the Theory of Scales of Measurement," *Science*, vol. 102 (1946), pp. 677–80.

4. For a detailed discussion of the MCA program, see Frank Andrews, James Morgan, and John Sonquist, *Multiple Classification Analysis* (Ann Arbor, Mich.: Survey Research Center, University of Michigan, 1969). For extensive applications, see James N. Morgan, M. David, W. Cohen, and H. Brazer, *Income and Welfare in the United States* (New York: McGraw-Hill, 1962); James N. Morgan, I. Sirageldin, and N. Baerwaldt, *Productive Americans* (Ann Arbor, Mich.: Survey Research Center, University of Michigan, 1966); and Ismail A. Sirageldin, *Non-Market Components of National Income* (Ann Arbor, Mich.: Survey Research Center, University of Michigan, 1969). For an early discussion of dummy variable regressions, see Daniel B. Suits, "Use of Dummy Variables in Regression Equations," *Journal of the American Statistical Association*, vol. 52 (1957), pp. 548–51.

5. Andrews, Morgan, and Sonquist, *Multiple Classification Analysis*, p. 10.

6. Andrews, Morgan, and Sonquist, *Multiple Classification Analysis*, pp. 95–106.

8. Geographic Mobility

AN IMPORTANT COMPONENT of the characteristics and dynamics of the labor supply is the geographic movement of labor in the kingdom. Particular attention is focused on the extent and determinants of interregional migration because of its significant policy implications. Given an expanding economy with substantial capital investment in almost all the socioeconomic sectors, and provided the system of labor market information functions reasonably well, labor is expected to respond to new opportunities by moving to areas that provide more employment and higher earnings. In such a context, labor mobility can be an effective mechanism to allocate the economy's labor force. Geographic mobility will tend to equalize labor returns among sectors and regions and promote efficient growth patterns. In general, geographic labor mobility may be conceptualized as both a factor in, and a consequence of, the modernization and growth of the economy. It introduces regional imbalances into the relationship between technological change and labor supply and demand and is also a force of demographic change. To the extent that migrants tend to be more enterprising than nonmigrants and to possess human capital characteristics that contribute relatively more to economic growth, they could be viewed as the most productive element in the population from which they moved. Conversely, and depending on the rate and structure of migration, mobility may also be responsible for uneven regional growth that may cause socioeconomic dislocations. The present study is therefore concerned with the impact of regional development on interregional labor mobility and vice versa.

In the analysis presented in this chapter, the survey findings will be used to address the following questions: What is the extent of labor mobility in Saudi Arabia? What is the extent of interregional migration? What is the likely extent of future mobility? What are the factors associated with such moves?

The answers to the first two questions are descriptive in nature; the answer to the third merely a report on respondents' views. Together, they provide policymakers with a basic profile of geographic labor mobility in the kingdom. Although descriptive, the information is a prerequisite for the more substantive analysis necessary to answer the last question, or for any attempt to understand the dynamics of the labor market. This is especially so in the present case since little is known about the extent and structure of past or current labor mobility in Saudi Arabia. A general profile of labor migration is presented in the second part of this chapter.

The last question is more analytic in character and also has greater policy relevance because the determinants of geographic labor mobility in Saudi Arabia have implications for various facets of social planning. There is, however, no simple and ready answer. One constraint on the analysis is that the cross-sectional nature of the survey data seriously limits dynamic interpretations. Another relates to the limited knowledge, conceptual and empirical, about the causes and consequences of the migration process in Saudi Arabia prior to the present study.[1] Accordingly, the multivariate analysis presented later in this chapter attempts to examine the determinants of geographic mobility, but should be viewed as only exploratory. It is a first step in the design of a more comprehensive study of the migration process. The focus is also largely on the Saudi segment of the labor force, as the geographical movement of most non-Saudi workers is restricted by contractual and legal arrangements.

The following discussion is divided into three parts. First, an introductory overview presents a profile of labor mobility and examines interregional mobility, plans to move, and the basic framework of determinants of geographic mobility. Second, the multivariate analysis is presented. Third, the results of the analysis are assessed. A brief conclusion summarizes the discussion and assesses some of the policy implications.

Overview

Profile of Labor Mobility

A first step in measuring labor mobility is to examine the length of stay by current place of residence. Among the sample of Saudi establishment workers, about 16 percent had lived in their current homes for less than one year and about 12 percent for one to three years. In other words, 28 percent of Saudi establishment workers had moved to their current place of residence during the three years preceding 1978. The mobility of the heads of Saudi households exhibited a similar pattern; there were some regional variations, however, especially among establishment workers. The extent of recent movement (that is, during the previous twelve months) was most apparent in the Central region (31 percent of the sample) and least in the Southern region (2 percent). Paradoxically, the

Central region showed the smallest recent movement for households during the previous twelve months (5 percent), while the Southern region showed the highest movement (14 percent). The extent of movement for non-Saudi workers was more substantial. For example, almost 72 percent of the establishment non-Saudi workers had moved to their current residence during the previous three years; about 31 percent had moved during the previous twelve months. Again, there seems to have been significant regional differences, with more recent moves reported in the Northern and Southern regions, possibly because of recent development efforts. One must nevertheless be cautious when interpreting these rates because of the small number of cases surveyed in these two regions. The pattern, however, was similar for the non-Saudi household sample, and this should provide some confidence in the general findings.

Interregional Mobility

The significant, although not substantial, residential mobility in the Saudi labor force raises an important question: How much of this movement is between regions? The findings, in fact, indicated very little interregional migration. Among those Saudi workers or heads of households who had moved during the previous twelve months, at least 80 percent had moved within their current region of residence. Therefore, only about 3 percent of the total Saudi labor force had moved between regions during the previous twelve months. The case of Saudi establishment workers in the Northern region is an exception, as only 25 percent of the sample reported moving within their own region. This finding, however, cannot be sustained with confidence because of the small number of responses in that region (only eight persons reported moving). When more migration cases were reported, as in the household sample in the same Northern region, the proportion of out-regional migration tends to decline and converges to the general tendency. The previous findings are further confirmed when the last move, regardless of its date, is examined: almost all such movements originated either from outside Saudi Arabia or within the same region.

What are the reasons for the apparent lack of interregional migration? Such a question cannot be answered fully from a single cross-sectional survey. An important factor, however, could be individual preferences for working in a given region. Most of the Saudi respondents in both samples again indicated their preference for work in the region in which they lived. There was a slight preference for working in the Western region, especially as indicated by people living in the Northern and the

Southern regions (14 and 8 percent of the sample, respectively). Even in these two regions the majority indicated a decided preference for their current residence (74 and 88 percent, respectively).

Plans to Move

Undoubtedly, mobility, regardless of its relative size, is a recent phenomenon among the Saudi labor force. Whether such mobility becomes substantial will depend on the response of Saudi workers to spatial incentives and opportunities. If this response exists at all, it will most likely lag in time, possibly because of deep-rooted traditions related to family structure and to a value system that increases individuals' cost of moving. It is also possible that the market itself did not provide either the necessary information about alternative opportunities or the necessary incentives to make a move worthwhile. From this perspective, analysis of plans to move should give some assessment of potential mobility and be less susceptible to the lagged response, at least to some extent. The proportion of Saudi workers or heads of household who intend to move is not sizable, varying between 2 and 16 percent, and most of the planned destinations are within the current region of residence. As expected, planned moves were less frequent for the non-Saudi labor force, partly because of contractual rules. Even then, most of the planned moves were within the region.

Determinants of Geographic Mobility

In view of the findings that there is no substantial interregional labor movement in Saudi Arabia and that most of the limited movement has been within regions, some pertinent questions arise: Is it possible to establish some systematic pattern for such apparent limited labor migration? Is it possible, for example, to identify what types of population groups are more or less likely to move? These are clearly important policy questions. For example, if the pattern of labor migration appears to be systematic rather than random, it will be more predictable. Accordingly, it will be more likely to be influenced by policy. Furthermore, such findings should give more credence to the study findings in general.

A thorough analysis of the causes and consequences of labor migration in Saudi Arabia is beyond the scope of this analysis, which seeks only to identify the effects of some factors viewed as important in the process of migration or relevant to social policy. The analysis will be limited to the Saudi segment of the labor force since the geographic movement of most non-Saudi workers is very largely restricted by contractual and legal arrangements. Interregional mobility will not be examined as a separate phenomenon because of its relatively infrequent occurrence. Accordingly, the purpose of the analysis is to examine some of the determinants of the three aspects of geographic mobility of Saudi labor: plans to move, recent past geographic mobility (move occurring during the previous twelve months), and past geographic mobility (move occurring during the previous five years, excluding the previous twelve months).

The means (proportions) of these three dependent variables are presented in table 8-1. Each variable takes the value one if mobility occurred (or was planned) and zero otherwise. For each variable a multivariate model is specified and tested empirically. The specifications of the models are guided by general theoretical considerations related to the study as a whole. More theoretical discussion specific to the case of geographical migration is given below. It must be emphasized, however, that because of the pioneering nature of this investigation, the lack of a generally acceptable theoretical framework, and the special nature of the Saudi labor market, there is no strict adherence to a single theoretical proposition. Indeed, of the various models that attempt to explain labor migration, each has a different policy perspective, emphasis, and implications.[2]

Multivariate Analysis: The Framework

Theory and Methodology

There are at least four ways to approach the process of migration: through socioeconomic characteristics, subjective considerations, spatial

Table 8-1. *Indicators of Geographic Mobility*

Indicator	Establishment sample		Household sample	
	Sample size	Relevant percent	Sample size	Relevant percent
Plan to move	878	17.4	481	13.1
Recent past geographical mobility (moved during previous twelve months)	1,018	14.6	531	13.4
Past geographical mobility (moved during previous five years, excluding previous twelve months)	1,018	33.1	531	28.4

factors, and economic or cost-benefit calculations.[3] Migrants tend to be distinguishable by such socioeconomic characteristics as age, marital status, family size, education, and occupation.[4] The nature of such selectivity has implications for national and regional patterns of growth and development and for planning social services, such as housing, schooling, and health facilities. Subjective considerations refer to the personality traits and cultural factors that influence personal preferences, which in turn affect family orientation, the ranking of job location, or the extent of risk avoidance.[5] Spatial factors that influence the direction and magnitude of the migration movement include distance, information flows, and the presence of intervening opportunities.[6] The fourth approach relates to the role of economic forces, usually examined within a cost-benefit framework. In this context migration is considered to be one way of investing in human capital. A move implies various cost-benefit calculations and will take place if the present value of the stream of expected returns exceeds that of expected costs.[7] The problem reduces to a quantitative assessment of the various pecuniary and nonpecuniary elements of these costs and benefits and to the choice of an appropriate rate of discount. It could be argued that a general subjective cost-benefit framework may subsume all four aspects of the migration process if it is adequately specified. For example, a cost-benefit framework for migration analysis may be presented as follows:

$$M_{ij} = M_{ij} \left\{ \sum_{t=1}^{n} \frac{R_j^t}{(1+r)^t} - \sum_{t=1}^{n} \frac{C_i^t}{(1+r)^t} \right\} \tag{8.1}$$

$$R_j = R_j \, (I_{jn}, \, P_j, \, S_j, \, U_j, \, A_j, \, Z_j) \tag{8.2}$$

$$C_i = C_i \, (I_{in}, \, P_i, \, S_i, \, U_{iY}, \, A_i, \, Z_i, \, T_{ij}) \tag{8.3}$$

where M_{ij} = migration from place i to j
R_j = net returns at destination j
C_i = net cost incurred on leaving place i
r = discount rate on future earnings
t = time dimension $(t = 1, 2, \ldots n)$
n = total number of years in which earnings at j are expected, and for a portion of which some costs at i may continue (for example, supporting relatives)
I_{jn} = earnings potential at destination j specific to age of migrants; the same for I_{in} at destination i
P_j = profile of price, or cost of living, at j; the same for P_i at i
S_j = earnings potential specific to skills at j; similarly for S_i at i
U_j = risk of unemployment at j; similarly for U_i at i

A_j = nonmonetary and psychic benefits and amenities at j; similarly for A_i at i

Z_j = additional socioeconomic factors that may operate to condition the values taken on by I_j; similarly for Z_i at i

T_{ij} = cost of moving from place i to j.

According to the model, a decision to migrate from place i to place j is predicted when $M_{ij} = M_{ij}[(R_j) - (C_i)] > Q$ (some threshold value).[8]

It is evident that application of a model of this type will require extensive data well beyond those available. Optimally, it requires data collected for the same individuals at two points in time. In the present study data are collected for a given point in time. In addition, mobility is defined with reference to current residence only and as a dummy variable, a probability which takes the value of one if the individual has moved (or plans to move) and zero otherwise. The operational models specified below include indicators of the pecuniary and nonpecuniary factors that influence such probabilities. The general model specified above will be used as a guiding paradigm only.

Model Specification

The following three models are specified for planned and past geographic mobility:

$$PLM = PLM\ (R,\ PPE,\ LS,\ LC,\ E,\ CT, \qquad (8.4)$$
$$FI,\ HO,\ LJ,\ IA,\ SR,\ RJL)$$

$$RPM = RPM\ (R,\ LS,\ A,\ E,\ FI,\ HO,\ IA) \qquad (8.5)$$

$$PM = PM\ (R,\ LS,\ A,\ E,\ FI,\ HO,\ IA) \qquad (8.6)$$

where PLM = planned migration, a dummy variable that takes the value of one if respondent plans to move from current residence and zero otherwise

R = region, a dummy variable that takes the value of one if in Central, Eastern, or Western regions and zero otherwise

PPE = public or private establishment, a dummy variable that takes the value of one if work is in a private establishment and zero otherwise

LS = level of skill, a dummy variable that takes the value of one for higher skills (professional, technical, administrative, managerial, clerical, sales, and service) and zero otherwise

LC = length of current contract, which takes one of the following values:

0, if no contract
1, if one-year term
2, if two-year term
3, if three-year term
4, if four-year or longer term

A = age, which takes one of the following values:

0, if under 20 years old
1, if 20–24
2, if 25–29
3, if 30–34
4, if 35–39
5, if 40–44
6, if 45–49
7, if 50–54
8, if 55–59
9, if 60 +

CS = number of children in school, which takes the actual number for its value

E = education, which takes one of the following values:

0, no schooling
1, elementary
2, intermediate
3, secondary
4, university or college
5, postgraduate

CT = current training, a dummy variable that takes the value of one if the individual is taking training and zero otherwise

FI = annual family income, which takes one of the following values:

1, less than SR5,000
2, SR5,000–SR14,999
3, SR15,000–SR24,999
4, SR25,000–SR34,999
5, SR35,000–SR44,999
6, SR45,000–SR54,999
7, SR55,000 or more

HO = home ownership, which takes the value of one if the individual owns a home and zero otherwise.

LJ = looking for a job, which takes the value of one if the individual is looking for a job and zero otherwise.

IA = income adequacy, which takes one of the following values:

> 1, far too little income
> 2, not quite adequate
> 3, adequate
> 4, more than adequate
> 5, much more than adequate

SR = satisfied with residence, which takes the value of one if satisfied and zero otherwise.

RJL = ranking of job location, which takes the scale of 1 to 5; 1 is the lowest in preference, and 5 the highest in preference.

RPM = recent past migration (during previous twelve months), a dummy variable that takes the value of one if moved and zero otherwise.

PM = past migration (during previous five years, excluding the previous twelve months), a dummy variable that takes the value of one if moved and zero otherwise.

Consider first the model for planned migration. The region variable (R) reflects differential opportunities. Its coefficient is expected to be positive because of an assumed preference for the Central, Western, and Eastern regions by comparison with the Northern and Southern regions. The establishment variable (PPE) is a proxy for relative job security between public and private enterprises. Its coefficient is expected to be positive. The skill variable (LS) is a proxy for market opportunities. Since a strong demand exists for all types of skills, it is difficult to predict a priori the sign of its coefficient, but it is not unreasonable to expect higher skills to be relatively more mobile than lower skills, and thus to expect a positive coefficient. The length of contract (LC) is another variable reflecting the cost of moving. Its coefficient is expected to be negative: the longer the contract, the lower the probability of a planned move. Age (A) reflects many factors, and its net effect on mobility is likely to be negative. Since age indicates the likely number of working years, the older the person, the lower the value of the expected earnings. Age also reflects the stage in the life cycle; an older person is likely to have more firmly established attitudes toward his or her living environment and a higher social status, both of which increase the opportunity cost of moving. The number of children in school (*CS*) increases the cost of relocation. Its coefficient is expected to be negative. Education (*E*) reduces the cost of information, increases the chance of employability, and raises aspiration levels. Its coefficient is expected to be positive. Enrollment in current training (*CT*) is indicative of a conscious attempt to invest in one's own human capital. Such a person is expected to take advantage of available opportunities, and the coefficient of the training variable is thus expected to be positive.

The effect of family income (*FI*) is the outcome of two mechanisms. The higher the income, the more likely the head of household is to be responsive to the market signals and hence to move. This is also true if he perceives opportunities to get better housing and a more desirable living environment. Under these circumstances *FI* would be positively related to income: the higher the income, the higher the probability of moving. But, as discussed earlier, there are costs of moving, such as the opportunity cost of lost income, especially if the move includes a change in job or unpaid moving time. This cost, or price factor, is negatively related to income: the higher the income, the higher the potential loss. The final outcome of the relationship between income and mobility will depend on the relative strength of these two forces. Thus the coefficient of family income cannot be predicted a priori.

Income adequacy (*IA*) is another case where the coefficient cannot be predicted a priori because of the existence of two opposing mechanisms. If an adequate income is one that covers perceived necessary expenses, then income adequacy implies the ability to afford a move (the income effect is positive). On the other hand, a move may imply giving up some of the factors which contribute to this adequacy, for example, wages or living environment (the substitution or price effect is negative). In the context of the present analysis, where most moves are within limited geographical areas, it is plausible that the income effect would prevail; that is, *IA* would likely have a positive coefficient.

Home ownership (*HO*) is viewed as a major constraint on mobility, especially when housing is expensive. It is expected to have a negative coefficient. If a person is looking for a job (*LJ*), there is a significant probability that a new job will be sufficiently distant from the current residence that a move will be necessary. Its coefficient is expected to be positive. Satisfaction with current residence (*SR*) is taken as a subjective cost element. In a traditional environment it could have a strong negative effect on mobility. Another attitudinal factor is the respondent's ranking of the importance of job location (*RJL*). Its coefficient is expected to be negative.

The specifications for the two equations of past mobility are similar and include fewer variables than that of planned mobility. The justification for excluding some of the variables is self-evident because of the time reference.

Estimation Techniques

An estimation of the above models by using ordinary least squares is inappropriate for a number of technical considerations. A probit technique of the kind outlined in the appendix to this chapter was therefore used to derive the results presented in the following section.

Multivariate Analysis: The Results

The results of the multivariate analysis are presented in tables 8-2 to 8-4. In each table the findings for the establishment sample are presented first for the full model as specified initially and then in a short form that retains only the significant variables and a few others. The same procedure is applied to the household sample, and the findings are reported in the last two columns of each table. In each cell, the probit estimate is provided and a t-statistic is given below in parentheses. A t-value of 1.960 or more indicates significance at 0.05 or better. At the bottom of each column of the table the number of cases, the mean of the dependent variables, the degrees of freedom, and a χ^2 statistic (twice log likelihood) are provided. First, we examine the findings for plans to move and then past mobility.

Plans to Move

In the case of the establishment worker full model, three explanatory variables turned out to be significant: education, home ownership, and satisfaction with residence. As expected, education is positively related to moving plans, while home ownership and satisfaction with residence are negatively related. Satisfaction with residence, an attitudinal factor, seems to be the most significant factor affecting plans to move. It indicates that if individuals are satisfied with their current residence, the probability of planning to move is very significantly reduced. Life cycle variables (age and number of children in school) seem to have no significant effect on plans to move. A second analysis was done with a short form that retains the three significant explanatory variables and another five (skill level, family income, looking for a job, income adequacy, and ranking of job location). The results are reported in the second column of table 8-2. No significant change occurs in any of the coefficients. The findings seem to be robust, at least for this sample.

In the case of the household sample the same model was applied and the findings reported in the last two columns of table 8-2. Some differences exist in the results of the two samples. The common significant variables are home ownership and satisfaction with residence, and they have the expected negative coefficients. These two variables also have the highest levels of significance within their respective samples. Note that both variables are residence related, and they appear to be the most dominant factors affecting the Saudis' plan to move; all other variables, if significant, are so only at a lower level and are not common factors in both samples. Of the four significant variables found in the household sample, the remaining are level of skill and ranking of job location. The level of skill seems to be more important than education, as it shows the expected positive coefficient, while education shows no significant effect. The respondents' ranking of job location is another attitudinal variable which was found significant with the expected negative coefficient. When the shorter form of the model was applied (last column of table 8-2), neither the size nor the sign of the coefficients changed significantly for the four significant explanatory variables: level of skill, home ownership, satisfaction with residence, and ranking of job location. The goodness of the overall fit did not fall significantly (for example, the χ^2 reduced from 85 to 83 only).

Past Mobility

When recent and past geographic mobility were examined, a very small number of respondents turned out to have moved outside the boundaries of the city of residence (that is, there was little intercity or interregional mobility). Analysis of such an insignificant portion of those who moved would have been meaningless. Furthermore, there is no theoretically established foundation to explain conceptually the limited overall mobility and its narrow spatial dimensions. However, seven variables were introduced in the geographic mobility model in an attempt to explain recent and past mobility.

The findings presented in tables 8-3 and 8-4 show similarities between the results of the household sample and the establishment workers' sample for both the recent and past mobility models and regardless of whether the full or the short version of the model is used. In all eight cases age and home ownership were the only statistically significant variables,

Table 8-2. *Plan to Move: Saudi Establishment and Household Workers, 1978; Multivariate Analysis*
(probit estimates)

Variable	Establishment sample		Household sample	
	Full model	Reduced model	Full model	Reduced model
Intercept	−1.131	−1.207	0.101	0.276
	(−2.577)	(−3.086)	(0.142)	(0.451)
Region	−0.043	—	0.250	—
	(−.221)	—	(1.181)	—
Public/private establishment	0.142	—	—	—
	(1.001)	—	—	—
Level of skill	0.109	0.110	0.586	0.569
	(0.811)	(0.829)	(2.238)	(2.209)
Length of contract	−0.000	—	0.033	—
	(−0.003)	—	(0.189)	—
Age	−0.020	—	−0.024	—
	(−0.559)	—	(−0.415)	—
Number of children in school	−0.037	—	−0.022	—
	(−0.902)	—	(−0.455)	—
Education	0.123	0.164	0.074	0.114
	(2.236)	(3.291)	(0.941)	(1.644)
Current training	0.187	—	0.134	—
	(0.738)	—	(0.537)	—
Family income	0.044	0.020	0.060	0.049
	(1.130)	(0.569)	(1.002)	(0.855)
Home ownership	−0.405	−0.423	−0.577	−0.636
	(−3.289)	(−3.561)	(−3.247)	(−3.731)
Looking for job	0.187	0.197	−0.310	−0.280
	(1.464)	(1.547)	(−1.116)	(−1.019)
Income adequacy	0.089	0.101	−0.064	−0.095
	(1.210)	(1.380)	(−0.532)	(−0.818)
Satisfaction with residence	−.944	−0.916	−0.994	−0.989
	(−7.362)	(−7.315)	(−5.495)	(−5.535)
Rank: job location	0.075	0.065	−0.126	−0.133
	(1.864)	(1.675)	(−2.077)	(−2.233)
Number of observations	878	878	481	481
Mean dependent variable	0.174	0.174	0.131	0.131
Degrees of freedom	14	8	13	8
χ^2	74.8	70.1	85.3	83.0

— Not applicable.
Note: *t*-statistics in parentheses.

Table 8-3. *Moved during the Previous Twelve Months: Saudi Establishment and Household Workers, 1978; Multivariate Analysis* (probit estimates)

Variable	Establishment sample		Household sample	
	Full model	Reduced model	Full model	Reduced model
Intercept	−0.667	−0.601	−0.635	−0.551
	(−1.940)	(−4.140)	(−1.171)	(−1.955)
Region	−0.035	—	−0.018	—
	(−.213)	—	(−1.108)	—
Level of skill	0.006	—	−0.074	—
	(0.050)	—	(−0.409)	—
Age	−0.055	−0.055	−0.092	−0.092
	(−2.148)	(−2.140)	(−2.421)	(−2.431)
Education	0.056	0.056	−0.044	−0.052
	(1.155)	(1.245)	(−0.610)	(−0.751)
Family income	0.051	−0.052	0.052	0.049
	(1.481)	(1.516)	(1.046)	(1.031)
Home ownership	−0.468	−0.472	−0.540	−0.539
	(−4.174)	(−4.253)	(−3.739)	(−3.759)
Income adequacy	0.010	—	0.014	—
	(0.143)	—	(0.132)	—
Number of observations	1,018	1,018	531	531
Mean dependent variable	0.146	0.146	0.134	0.134
Degrees of freedom	7	4	7	4
χ^2	37.3	37.2	25.6	25.4

— Not applicable.
Note: *t*-statistics in parentheses.

and both have the expected negative coefficients. These findings are both important and conceptually meaningful. Age implies acquired prestige and social contacts within the residential environment. The sociopsychological cost of moving for the elderly, especially in the context of a traditional extended family, should therefore be high. Associated with this framework is home ownership since it implies not only the opportunity cost of relocation but also the social prestige associated with owning a home in the local environment.

Conclusions

Before we turn to the policy implications of the above findings, it is important to assess the quality of those findings. A systematic pattern of

Table 8-4. *Moved during the Previous Five Years: Saudi*
Establishment and Household Workers, 1978; Multivariate Analysis
(probit estimates)

Variable	Establishment sample		Household sample	
	Full model	Reduced model	Full model	Reduced model
Intercept	0.032	−0.244	−0.539	−0.245
	(0.114)	(−1.967)	(−1.190)	(−1.046)
Region	−0.094	—	−0.176	—
	(−0.720)	—	(−1.312)	—
Level of skill	0.080	—	0.014	—
	(0.823)	—	(0.093)	—
Age	−0.056	−0.056	−0.070	−0.073
	(−2.644)	(−2.691)	(−2.243)	(−2.356)
Education	−0.034	−0.021	0.107	0.098
	(−0.848)	(−0.571)	(1.783)	(1.688)
Family income	0.031	0.034	0.003	−0.013
	(1.092)	(1.194)	(0.081)	(−0.036)
Home ownership	−0.372	−0.356	−0.356	−0.354
	(−4.205)	(−4.079)	(−2.875)	(−2.894)
Income adequacy	−0.037	—	0.084	—
	(−0.682)	—	(0.966)	—
Number of observations	1,018	1,018	531	531
Mean dependent variable	0.331	0.331	0.284	0.284
Degrees of freedom	7	4	7	4
χ^2	30.1	28.4	33.4	30.0

— Not applicable.
Note: *t*-statistics in parentheses.

geographic mobility—whether in the past, present, or future—emerges from what now appears to be a reliable set of data. The study findings are compatible with both the theoretical constructs and other empirical findings reported in the literature. The explanatory variables show their expected signs for the two independent surveys of establishment and household workers. The two samples show similar, though not identical, results, and differences between the two can be explained. Furthermore, the results are generally robust; that is, when the short form of the model is used, the initially significant variables remain unchanged in sign or size of coefficient. For all these reasons, we can have confidence in the data and results obtained.

The significant variables in explaining recent and past mobility are, as indicated above, age and home ownership. As an explanation of plans to move, although home ownership appears significant in both samples, age does not. In the establishment sample other factors, such as education and satisfaction with residence, figure prominently. In the household sample, the skill level, satisfaction with residence, and ranking of job location appear to be the significant explanatory variables (in addition to home ownership). Since the goal is to design appropriate policies with maximum effectiveness, which of these variables are "policy-sensitive"; that is, which are susceptible to the influence of changes in policy?

Some variables are directly policy-sensitive; others, indirectly. Variables such as education, skill formation, and home ownership are directly policy-sensitive. The first two have positive coefficients while home ownership has a negative coefficient. If the authorities want to encourage labor flows, particularly of Saudis, to specific areas—for example, Jubail or Yanbu—to carry out large development projects, it is thus recommended that housing facilities as well as education and training services be generously extended to those areas to attract the target population.

The relation between policy and the other variables needs some elaboration. Age, looking for a job, satisfaction with residence, and ranking of job location may not appear to be policy-sensitive but in reality they are, albeit indirectly. The style, pace, and structure of development are all policy-related. An emphasis on opening employment opportunities for all age groups could influence the age distribution of the labor force as different age groups move into the new jobs. To the extent that dissemination of information facilitates the process of job search, government policy can affect individual plans for mobility by changing some information-related parameters. Even satisfaction with residence and ranking of job location, which appear to be especially limiting factors in the plans to move among households, can be influenced by government policies, though, understandably, not in the short term. Modernity, itself a function of development and government expenditures, will, in the long run, change neighborhoods and localities and thus affect satisfaction with residence and ranking of job location—two factors inhibiting geographic mobility, especially in the Saudi context.

Appendix. Probit Technique

The use of ordinary least squares is inappropriate for estimating the models described in the preceding text, not only because of problems associated with heteroscedasticity but also because there is nothing to constrain the dependent variable to the unit interval,[9] since a linear regression line, when fitted to the data, will predict values for the dependent variable that may exceed one or be less than zero. The probit technique is therefore used in the analysis.[10]

The probit model implies that the "probability of success" (in the current case, the probability of having moved or planning to move) can be written as:

$$E(y|x) = P(x) = (1/\sqrt{2\pi}) \int_{-\infty}^{x'\beta} \exp\left\{\frac{-U^2}{2}\right\} dU$$

$$= F(x'\beta)$$

where y is the binary variable, x a vector of explanatory variables, B a vector of parameters to be estimated, E the expected value of y given x, $P(x)$ the probability of having moved or of planning to move, and $F(\cdot)$ the cumulative normal distribution function. From the above model it is possible to obtain the maximum-likelihood estimating equations, and this system of nonlinear equations could be solved to obtain the maximum-likelihood estimates. It should be noted that $\partial P/\partial x_i$—the effect of a unit change in an explanatory variable on the dependent variable (the probability of success)—depends on the particular value of the vector of explanatory variables.

More formally,

$$\frac{\partial P}{\partial x_i} = \frac{\partial F(x\beta)}{\partial x_i} = F'(x'\beta) \cdot \beta_i.$$

Two additional points need mentioning. A correlation matrix indicates no serious correlation among the explanatory variables used in the analysis. A second concern refers to the possibility that looking for a job and plans to move are determined simultaneously. Also, past mobility may have influenced the independent variables of the equation over time. If so, parameter estimates are likely to possess a simultaneity bias. In the current analysis, it is assumed that such a bias is minimal.

Notes

1. For a review, see Paul Shaw, *Migration Theory and Fact: A Review* (Philadelphia, Penn.: Regional Science Institute, 1976).

2. See, for example, the taxonomy in Shaw, *Migration Theory and Fact*, pp. 13–15.

3. There is also the probabilistic approach that includes various stochastic models in which the interest is mainly to establish relationship. See, for example, the work of Robert McGinnis, "A Stochastic Model of Social Mobility," *American Sociological Review*, vol. 33 (1968), pp. 712–22.

4. See, for example, D. S. Thomas, "Age and Economic Differentials in Interstate

Migration," *Population Index* (1958), pp. 313–66; K. E. Taeuber, "Cohort Migration," *Demography*, vol. 3 (1966), pp. 416–23; P. M. Blau and O. D. Duncan, *The American Occupational Structure* (New York: Wiley, 1967); and Jack Landinsky, "The Geographical Mobility of Professional and Technical Manpower," *Journal of Human Resources*, vol. 2 (1967), pp. 475–95.

5. See, for example, J. S. Brown, H. K. Schwarzweller, and J. J. Magalam, "Kentucky Mountain Migration and the Stem Family," in C. J. Jansen, ed., *Readings in the Sociology of Migration* (New York: Pergamon, 1970), pp. 93–120.

6. See, for example, R. L. Morrill, "The Distribution of Migration Distances," *Papers of the Regional Science Association*, vol. 2 (1963), pp. 75–84; R. L. Morrill and E. R. Pitts, "Marriage, Migration and the Mean Information Field," *Annals of the Association of American Geographers*, vol. 57 (1967), pp. 401–22; and Brown, Schwarzweller, and Magalam, "Kentucky Mountain Migration."

7. See, for example, L. A. Sjaastad, "Income and Migration in the United States," Ph.D. dissertation, University of Chicago, 1961; T. W. Schultz, "Reflections on Investment in Man," *Journal of Political Economy*, vol. 70 (1962), pp. 51–57; L. E. Gallaway, "Industry Variation in Geographic Labor Mobility Patterns," *Journal of Human Resources*, vol. 2 (1967), pp. 461–74; M. J. Greenwood, "The Economics of Labor Mobility: An Empirical Analytical Comment," *Western Economic Journal*, vol. 6 (1968), pp. 243–44; Bernard Okun, "Interstate Population and State Income Inequality: A Simultaneous Equation Approach," *Economic Development and Cultural Change*, vol. 16 (1968), pp. 279–315; and M. P. Todaro, "A Model of Labor Migration and Urban Unemployment," *American Economic Review*, vol. 69 (1969), pp. 183–93.

8. For more details, see Shaw, *Migration Theory and Fact*, pp. 865–89.

9. See, for example, A. S. Goldberger, *Econometric Theory* (New York: Wiley, 1964), p. 249; or Henry Theil, *Principles of Econometrics* (New York: Wiley, 1971), pp. 628–36.

10. For a more detailed discussion of probit analysis, the reader is referred to James Tobin, "The Application of Multivariate Probit Analysis to Economic Survey Data," Cowles Foundation Discussion Paper no. 1 (New Haven, Conn.: Yale University, 1955); D. J. Finney, *Probit Analysis* (Cambridge, Eng.: Cambridge University Press, 1952); and S. M. Goldfield and R. E. Quandt, *Nonlinear Methods in Econometrics* (Amsterdam: North-Holland, 1972). For subsequent applications of the probit technique, see Ismail Sirageldin, M. Ali Khan, Ayse Ariturk, and Farida Shah, "Fertility Decisions and Desires in Bangladesh: An Econometric Investigation," *Bangladesh Development Studies*, vol. 4 (1970), pp. 329–50; and M. Ali Khan and Ismail Sirageldin, "Son Preference and the Demand for Children in Pakistan," *Demography*, vol. 14 (1976), pp. 481–96; and, by the same authors, "Education, Income, and Fertility in Pakistan," *Economic Development and Cultural Change*, vol. 27, no. 3 (1979), pp. 519–47.

9. Job, Occupational, and Sectoral Mobility

OCCUPATIONAL AND SECTORAL MOBILITY are indicators of the extent to which labor adapts to changing market conditions. Where the development process is accelerated without significant constraints on capital availability, the outcome of development will depend to a large degree on the availability of labor and on the pace of its adjustment to continuously changing conditions.

In Saudi Arabia various forces influence the process of labor adaptation in opposite directions. For a time, with the almost open-ended policy of importing expatriate labor, coupled with what seemed to be an undiminished supply of labor from neighboring countries or from farther afield, there was little pressure on, or need for, local labor to accelerate its own pace of market adaptation. Furthermore, in the initial phase, large-scale construction of infrastructure may not have needed the highly specialized technology which requires on-the-job training or retraining and increases the cost of intersectoral and interoccupational labor mobility.

Labor response, however, is a function not only of changing demand conditions but also of supply characteristics as well as of the structure of the labor market itself. The mechanism providing information on job availability, the pattern of contractual arrangements, on-the-job training, and nonwage benefits are but some of the relevant characteristics that should influence the rate of occupational mobility. On the supply side three specific characteristics of Saudi workers may influence the elasticity of labor mobility: preference for special sectors and occupations (for example, government jobs); resistance to the discipline required by modern organizations (for example, regular working hours); and preference for independence from external authority (for example, through self-employment).

These characteristics are frequently mentioned as determinants of occupational mobility in a growing economy. As such, they must be parametrically integrated into any comprehensive manpower development policy. In Saudi Arabia, however, empirical evidence has hitherto been lacking not only about such factors and their relationships to mobility, but more fundamentally about the extent of occupational mobility itself.

In this chapter the rate of sectoral and occupational mobility in the five regions for both Saudi and non-Saudi labor will be examined. This profile will then serve as the basis for the subsequent detailed analysis of the possible causes of occupational mobility in the kingdom. As in chapter 8, this latter analysis will be limited to the Saudi segment of the labor force.

This chapter is accordingly divided into three parts. The first presents an overview of occupational mobility. The second presents a framework for the multivariate analysis, and the third the results of that analysis. There is a brief concluding summary and discussion of policy implications.

Overview

Occupational Mobility

As a first step, the change from the initial to the most recent employment is examined. Workers who are in their first jobs are excluded from the analysis; thus, 43 percent of the Saudi workers were excluded (455 out of a total independent household sample of 1,049). The findings are available for all regions and indicate substantial occupational mobility of the Saudi workers in all occupational groups, except that of production and operative labor. The proportion of those who changed occupations varied from about 72 percent for sales and services to 66 percent for administrative and managerial, to 56 percent for professional and technical, and to 42 percent for clerical occupations. For production and operative labor, occupational mobility was only 22 percent.

Upward mobility for Saudi workers was significant. For example, 28 percent of the professional/technical group had previously worked in the clerical category and the same was almost true for the administrative/ managerial personnel; 21 percent of the clerical and 32 percent of the sales workers were previously production/operative labor. This general picture does not change significantly when examined at the regional level, although here the number of cases was too small to provide confidence in the estimates.

To what extent is the pattern of occupational mobility among the establishment workers similar to that of the independent household sample? Such a comparison should give confidence in the findings. One must be careful, however, since an important reason for sampling the households was to obtain a more detailed picture of the traditional occupations and activities in the labor market, and one would thus expect a different occupational mix. The findings for the Saudi household sample exclude about 57 percent of all cases (490 out of 864) because the current job was the respondent's first.

The extent of mobility in the household sample was at least as substantial as in the case of establishment workers. It varied from a high 92 percent for sales, 82 percent for administrative/managerial, 80 percent for service, 56 percent for clerical, and 50 percent for professional/ technical, to 49 percent for production/operative labor. The mobility of the production/operative labor category in the sample of households was more than double that in the sample of the establishment workers. A more interesting finding was that among those heads of household whose current employment was production and operative labor, 21 percent had a previous job in agriculture or animal husbandry. The findings also indicate a general pattern of upward mobility. In general, these mutually supporting results from two independent surveys give more confidence in the finding of substantial occupational mobility among the Saudi labor force during the period of the study.

The picture for non-Saudi establishment workers is somewhat different. For this group 33 percent of the cases were excluded (278 out of 830). Occupational mobility was, as expected, lower than that of the Saudi workers, but it was not insignificant. It varied from 68 percent for sales workers, 52 percent for administrative/managerial, 45 percent for service, to 22 percent for production/operative labor, and 18 percent for professional/technical. There was some apparent downward mobility, especially among the production/operative labor for the sample of non-Saudi heads of household.

Planned Job Change

It is possible that past occupational mobility was a result of the accelerated pace of development that occurred in the mid-1970s. That peak has subsequently passed, and the question is: how much future occupational mobility is expected? As already noted, a developing society moves from constructing its infrastructure to developing more modern sectors which require more specialized skills; as a result, occupational mobility becomes more costly for both employers and employees. One crude estimate of the extent of future mobility is "planned change of job." About 16 percent of Saudi workers in public establishments indicated definite plans to change jobs, and a further 14 percent had probable plans. These proportions were significantly lower for Saudis in private establishments

and for heads of household. There are apparent differences among
regions, especially for Saudis in public establishments, but in general
there is a correspondence between Saudi household plans and the average establishment worker's plans, with the exception of the Northern and
Southern regions.

Determinants of Occupational and Sectoral Mobility

The basic determinants of occupational mobility among the Saudi
labor force and their policy implications are the two main themes that will
now be investigated. Given the Saudi labor market's unique structural
characteristics, the present analysis should be viewed as largely exploratory. First, some basic propositions regarding the determinants of occupational mobility are offered as the basis for the specification of the
subsequent multivariate analysis. To narrow the scope of the investigation and focus on its policy implications, the analysis will be limited to the
Saudi segment of the labor force and will apply to the kingdom as a whole
rather than to component regions. More specifically, the purpose of the
analysis is to examine some of the determinants of four indicators of
occupational mobility for Saudi labor: looking for a job; recent occupational mobility (change in occupation during the previous two years); past
occupational mobility (change in occupation during the previous four
years); and recent change in industry (during the previous two years).
Recent occupational mobility is defined as having occurred within two
years because of the small number of cases associated with changes
during the previous twelve months, which was the basis of the definition
for recent geographic mobility as discussed in the preceding chapter. If
those few cases had been used, they would have produced a rather
unstable pattern.

The means (proportion) of these four dependent variables are presented in table 9-1. Each variable takes the value one if mobility occurred
(or was planned) and zero otherwise. For the three cases of past mobility
only those workers who had a previous job were included. Each of these
four indicators takes the form of a dependent variable in a multivariate
model which is specified and tested empirically. The specifications of the
models are guided by some general theoretical considerations, which will
now be discussed.

Theory and Methodology

A discussion of occupational mobility is embedded in the problem of
wage formation, which in turn implies the study of dynamics of the supply

Table 9-1. *Indicators of Occupational Mobility*

Indicator	Establishment sample		Household sample	
	Sample size	Relevant percent	Sample size	Relevant percent
Looking for job	969	19.5	499	9.8
Change in occupation previous two years	583	18.5	269	11.9
Change in occupation previous four years	583	26.6	269	17.8
Change in industry previous two years	543	36.5	241	12.4

of and demand for labor. There are many reasons that such a dynamic mechanism may be set in motion. The level and composition of the demand for final and intermediate products in Saudi Arabia are undergoing continuous change as a result of the recent dramatic increase in both government expenditures and in the real income of consumers and their consumption habits. The demand for labor also stems from the changes in production techniques that require different qualities of labor. Determinants of labor supply include the education and training system, the job search information system, and workers' preferences between work and leisure. It is evident that in order to understand the causes of and the motives for job changes, one needs to understand the real and perceived differences between the various jobs. For example, the transfer of manpower from one sector to another may be a result of differences in their rates of expansion and in the implied labor-output ratios. In this context, labor may move from a contracting sector to an expanding sector when different wage rates are paid for the same type of job in the two sectors. When the difference is small, wage earners are probably "pushed" away from the contracting sectors (firms), for example, by layoffs. When the difference is large, they are probably "pulled" by expectations of higher wages in the expanding sectors (firms). The same description would probably also hold for the differential in perceived opportunities for advancement.

This general view of labor market dynamics provides the basic framework for most of the formal analysis of occupational mobility.[1] It assumes that, given some normal rate of labor turnover, most of the occupational mobility is based on some conscious calculations by the workers; that is, they respond rationally to perceived signals. Earlier findings presented in this book, however, indicate that some factors in the Saudi context, which are conducive to additional dynamic behavior, may not necessarily be so completely calculated. Thus unemployment among Saudi workers is almost nonexistent, the result of an overheated economy, with no evidence that this strong demand for Saudi workers will slacken in the near future. When managers were asked about their business prospects, almost all expected some sort of expansion in their activities; very few expected contraction. Thus the wage differential hypothesis, if it applies in the Saudi market, would apply through the "pull" mechanism and not as a result of workers' layoffs. Given this very strong demand for Saudi labor, however, it is not evident a priori what role economic considerations play in formulating occupational mobility decisions as opposed to noneconomic considerations, such as traditional values and preferences for specific types of jobs or sectors. It is possible that in the current context a non-negligible part of mobility is quite independent of wage considerations and is rather haphazard (involving "floaters").

Occupational mobility may therefore be divided into four types:

- Mobility through the natural turnover of labor: young persons enter the labor market and elderly persons leave.
- Mobility through voluntary, rational deliberations: workers weigh differences in wages paid for different jobs and evaluate the various pecuniary costs, including the direct cost of moving; they also attach an element of expectations to those calculations to reflect the probable success or failure as, for example, the expected timing and duration of the net benefit.
- Mobility through involuntary, rational deliberation: those who move are from the supply of discarded workers; they decide on their new job, however, after rational evaluation of the various alternatives.
- Haphazard mobility of "floaters": workers who move from one job or firm to another without systematic regard to wage differential or other pecuniary or nonpecuniary rewards are probably more prevalent when the economy is strong and the demand for labor is accordingly high.

In the Saudi labor market the second and fourth types are the most relevant; unemployment seems to be insignificant under current conditions, and a study of natural turnover rates, although important, is not the main focus of this chapter.

A rational decision regarding a job change would imply a weighing of expected costs and benefits. As an illustration, consider the example of a wage earner's choice between moving or staying in his current job. Assume a two-period model. In the first period, T, wages and other amenities in the two job alternatives (W_1 and W_2) are known and fixed, for example, because of contractual arrangement. Thus, the wage differential during T is fixed at ($W_2 - W_1$). In the second period T' (that extends over the wage earner's planning horizon) wages and amenities are based on expectations. In this simplified example the expectation variable may take three values, implying three wage differentials. The first assumes that W_1 and W_2 remain unchanged and the differential also remains unchanged; that is, ($W_2 - W_1$) = ($W_2' - W_1'$). The second assumes that the wage in the old job increases, ($W_1' > W_1$), while the wage in the new job remains unchanged ($W_2' = W_2$); thus the wage differential becomes ($W_2' - W_1'$), which is lower than before; that is, ($W_2' - W_1'$) < ($W_2 - W_1$). The third implies an increase in the wage differential, thus ($W_2' - W_1'$) > ($W_2 - W_1$). A final factor in the decision process relates to the various expenses, trouble, and inconvenience resulting from changing employment (C).

We notice, however, that C is a function of various factors; it should be written as $C(Y)$, where the vector (Y), defining the cost of changing jobs, may include: direct financial costs; acquisition of new skills; additional formal training; temporary displacement in the work environment as current connections with colleagues and organizations are broken; loss of status or seniority; and costs related to geographical moves (examined in the previous chapter). Such decision processes may be summarized in the form of a subjective partition decision tree as illustrated in figure 9-1. In this highly simplified example there are four conceivable payoffs, numbered (1) to (4). In reality the number of alternatives is much greater, but those discussed here are the most relevant. For the move to be at all advantageous, payoff (4) must be larger than payoff (2), and the difference must exceed C. According to this framework a decision to change jobs (from i to j) is predicted when

$$OM_{ij} = OM_{ij}[W_{ij} - (C_j) > Q \text{ (some threshold value)}.$$

Based on the general conceptual framework just discussed, the following four models are specified for planned and past occupational mobility:

$$LFJ = LFJ \ (R, \ PPE, \ LS, \ LC, \ A, \ CS, \ E, \ CT, \qquad (9.1)$$
$$MS, \ HO, \ IA, \ IO, \ JS, \ BP, \ RJI)$$

$$ROM = ROM \ (R, \ PPE, \ LS, \ A, \ E, \ MS, \ HO, \ IA) \qquad (9.2)$$

$$POM = POM \ (R, \ PPE, \ LS, \ A, \ E, \ MS, \ HO, \ IA) \qquad (9.3)$$

$$RIM \ = RIM \ \ (R, \ PPE, \ LS, \ A, \ E, \ MS, \ HO, \ IA) \qquad (9.4)$$

Figure 9-1. *A Decision to Change Jobs: A Partition Tree*

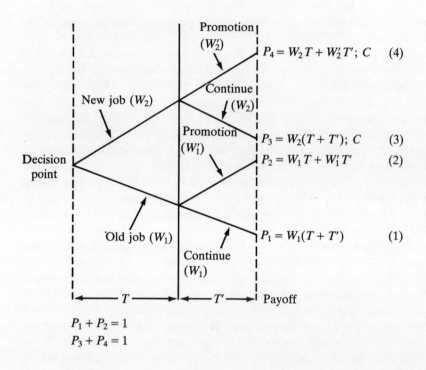

$$P_1 + P_2 = 1$$
$$P_3 + P_4 = 1$$

where LFJ = looking for job, a dummy variable that takes the value of one if the respondent is looking for a job and zero otherwise

ROM = recent occupation mobility, a dummy variable that takes the value of one if the respondent changed occupational status (based on the eight occupational categories) during the previous two years and zero otherwise

POM = past occupation mobility, a dummy variable that takes the value of one if the respondent changed occupational status (based on the eight occupational categories) during the previous four years and zero otherwise

RIM = recent industrial mobility, a dummy variable that takes the value of one if respondent changed industry during the previous two years and zero otherwise

R = region, a dummy variable that takes the value of one if in Central, Eastern, or Western regions and zero otherwise

PPE = public or private establishment, a dummy variable that takes the value of one if work is in a private establishment and zero otherwise

LS = level of skill, a dummy variable that takes the value of one for higher skills (professional, technical, administrative, managerial, clerical, sales, and service workers) and zero otherwise

CS = number of children in school, which takes the actual number for its value

CT = current training, a dummy variable that takes the value of one if the individual is taking training and zero otherwise

MS = monthly salary, which takes one of the following values:

1, less than SR1,000
2, SR1,000–SR1,499
3, SR1,500–SR1,999
4, SR2,000–SR2,999
5, SR3,000–SR4,999
6, SR5,000–SR7,499
7, SR7,500+

HO = home ownership, which takes the value of one if the individual owns a home, zero otherwise

IO = number of items owned, which takes as its value the actual number of vehicles and major appliances owned, which can range from zero to eight

JS = satisfaction with the current job, which takes the value of one if the individual is satisfied with his current job, zero otherwise

BP = better pay in job, which takes the value of one if the individual perceives he is getting a better pay than his peers, zero otherwise

RJI = ranking of job income, which takes the scale of one to five; one being the lowest in preference and five the highest in preference.

The following variables were defined in the preceding chapter:

LC = length of current contract, which takes a value of zero to four
A = age, which takes the value of zero to nine

E = education, which takes the value of zero to five

IA = income adequacy, which takes the value of one to five.

Consider first the model for looking for a job. The region variable (R) reflects differential opportunities. To the extent that there are more job opportunities available in the Central, Eastern, and Western regions, more job change is expected, both the rational, deliberate type of mobility and the haphazard. The coefficient is expected to be positive. In the case of past mobility, however, the region coefficient is expected to be negative since the process of development is more recent in the Northern and Southern regions. Workers, especially those in the establishment sample, were probably newcomers.

The public/private establishment (PPE) variable (limited to the analysis of the establishment sample) is a proxy for security and prestige. In a booming economy, with ever increasing incentives in the private sector, such factors may have no effect in current decisions. If such a value system existed, it should show in earlier mobility. The PPE coefficient is expected to be nonsignificant for looking for job but negative for past mobility.

The skill variable (LS) is a proxy for market opportunities. But because of the strong demand for all types of skill, it is not immediately clear what the sign of the coefficient will be. In the case of looking for a job two forces may be operating in opposite directions. By virtue of education and training the higher skill group has better access to information, which reduces the cost of identifying job alternatives. The lower skill group, however, may have been developing aspirations that motivate them to seek better opportunities. Furthermore, the incidence of floaters might be higher among the low-skilled group. The final outcome can be determined only empirically. In the case of past mobility, especially for the establishment sample, the coefficient is expected to be positive, mainly because of the reported high incidence of upward occupational mobility among the Saudi workers noted earlier.

Age (A) is expected to have a negative coefficient, especially in cases of past mobility. The number of children in school (CS) is another cost element that is expected to have a negative effect. Education, however, is expected to have a positive coefficient because more highly educated workers will have more market opportunities and alternatives; lower costs of job search, higher aspirations, and a longer planning horizon. Current training may influence occupational mobility in two opposite directions. On the one hand it increases the chances of employability, but on the other hand it implies an opportunity cost to the extent that it is relevant to advancement in the current job. Its coefficient may not be significant.

The ideal income variable to explain decisions regarding occupational mobility, according to the general conceptual framework discussed earlier, should have been the difference between the present value of the streams of current and expected earnings at the time of the decision. Such a theoretical construct does not exist in the present data set. Instead, in the model of looking for job, monthly salary (MS) serves as an indicator of relative success in current employment, other things being equal. The higher the wages, given age, education, and other socioeconomic characteristics, the higher the relative opportunity cost of moving. The coefficient of MS is thus expected to be negative for the case of looking for job. In models of past mobility the coefficient is also expected to be negative; the theoretical rationale, however, is different. Recent movers are expected to do better than if they had not moved; that is, to improve relative to their peers left in the old job situation. In general, however, movers are not expected to catch up with their peers in the new jobs. In the case of past mobility, MS measures the difference between wages of those who moved to the new job and wages of peers in that new job. We are facing, however, a problem of simultaneity: monthly salary is determined in part by past occupational mobility, yet, given expectations, monthly salary was itself a determining factor of mobility.

Home ownership (HO) is expected to be negatively related to occupational mobility to the extent that changing jobs might imply changing residence. Income adequacy includes two conflicting factors. If people have more than adequate income, they might afford the risk of trying new opportunities, whereas if they have a low income relative to perceived needs, they might search for alternative job opportunities. In the case of looking for a job, the coefficient for income adequacy is probably positive, since seeking information regarding new opportunity is an assessed factor, thus implying some cost. In the case of past mobility the outcome cannot be determined a priori.

A set of attitudinal variables was also included in the model for looking for a job: number of items owned (IO), job satisfaction (JS), better pay in current job (BP), and rank of job income (JI). The number of items owned, although it might reflect relative wealth, is taken in this analysis as an indicator of modernity. The presence of such items indicates a greater willingness to take steps to improve one's own living standards. The coefficient of IO is expected to be positive. Job satisfaction (JS) is an index of the nonpecuniary cost of leaving the current job; its coefficient is expected to be negative. A related factor is the individual's perception of whether he is adequately rewarded in the current job (BP), which also has an expected negative coefficient. An individual who gives a high ranking to income (RJI) among other job features, such as security and prestige, is expected to have an economic rationale for changing his job.

He is probably more prepared to evaluate and to respond to new opportunities; therefore the coefficient is expected to be positive. All the relations just described, although based on some plausible expectations of the dynamic movement of workers among various jobs and occupations, are clearly speculative and exploratory.

Multivariate Analysis: The Results

When the four models of occupational mobility are estimated, the same problem discussed in the previous chapter on geographic mobility crops up. All the dependent variables are binary and thus cannot be estimated adequately by using ordinary least squares. The probit technique was used instead. The results of the multivariate analysis are presented in tables 9-2 to 9-5. In each table the findings for the establishment sample are presented, first for the full model as specified above and then in a short form retaining only the significant variables and a few others viewed as important for conceptual and policy considerations. The same procedure is applied to the household sample and to the related findings reported in the last two columns of each table. Each cell of the table shows the probit estimate with its t-statistic in parentheses below it. A t-value of 1.960 or more indicates a significant level at 0.05 or better. At the bottom of each column of the table the number of cases, the mean of the variable, the degrees of freedom, and a χ^2 statistic (twice log likelihood) are provided. First, we examine the findings for looking for job, set out in table 9-2.

Looking for Job

In the case of the establishment worker full model, five explanatory variables turned out to be significant: region (R), home ownership (HO), income adequacy (IA), items owned (IO), and job satisfaction (JS). Education was close to being significant (t-statistic = 1.880). As expected, the coefficient is positive for region and negative for home ownership. The coefficient for income adequacy turned out to be highly significant and positive, which suggests that the effect of income adequacy prevailed: those who perceive their income to be adequate for their needs seem to afford the cost of obtaining information regarding job opportunities and to take steps in evaluating alternatives. Number of items owned (IO) as an index of modernity seems to work in the same direction: it has a significantly positive coefficient. As expected, satisfaction with current job increases the opportunity cost of leaving it. Its

Table 9-2. *Looking for Job: Saudi Establishment and Household Workers, 1978; Multivariate Analysis*
(probit estimates)

Variable	Establishment sample		Household sample	
	Full model	Reduced model	Full model	Reduced model
Intercept	−1.820	−1.863	−0.292	−0.415
	(−4.510)	(−4.822)	(−0.375)	(−0.556)
Region	0.420	0.416	0.173	0.191
	(2.080)	(2.282)	(0.714)	(0.806)
Public/private establishment	−0.043	—	—	—
	(−0.320)	—	—	—
Level of skill	0.180	—	0.231	—
	(1.540)	—	(0.948)	—
Length of contract	0.019	—	—	—
	(0.300)	—	—	—
Age	−0.009	−0.031	−0.066	−0.047
	(−0.290)	(−1.215)	(−1.104)	(−1.033)
Number of children in school	−0.044	—	0.009	—
	(−2.220)	—	(0.161)	—
Education	0.097	0.123	0.085	0.114
	(1.880)	(2.624)	(0.907)	(1.284)
Current training	0.012	—	−0.261	—
	(0.048)	—	(−0.768)	—
Monthly salary	−0.038	−0.049	−0.028	−0.039
	(−0.830)	(−1.091)	(−0.323)	(−0.475)
Home ownership	−0.230	−0.245	−0.279	−0.227
	(−2.120)	(−2.316)	(−1.500)	(−1.253)
Income adequacy	0.240	0.234	0.025	0.014
	(3.580)	(3.545)	(0.190)	(0.110)
Number of items owned	0.065	0.065	0.075	0.068
	(2.040)	(2.062)	(1.117)	(1.032)
Job satisfaction	−0.390	−0.386	−1.396	−1.447
	(−2.950)	(−2.966)	(−6.160)	(−6.554)
Better pay in current job	0.180	—	0.389	—
	(1.160)	—	(0.909)	—
Rank: job income	−0.023	—	−0.024	—
	(−0.550)	—	(−0.256)	—
Number of observations	969	969	499	499
Mean dependent variable	0.195	0.195	0.098	0.098
Degrees of freedom	15	8	13	8
χ^2	67.9	62.3	68.5	66.0

— Not applicable.

coefficient is negative and significant. The coefficient of education, although not significant at the 0.05 level, was positive as expected and became significant in the short model. In the short model, reported in the second column of table 9-2, the five significant explanatory variables were retained along with age, education, and monthly salary. There seems to be no significant change in any of the coefficients except education. Thus, the findings appear to be robust.

For the household sample, the same model and method were estimated and the findings reported in the third and fourth columns of table 9-2, with noticeable differences. The only significant explanatory variable is job satisfaction. The only variables that were somewhat close to significance were home ownership and education with the expected signs of coefficients. Other factors, although having the same signs for their coefficients as in the establishment sample, were not significant. These findings did not change when the short model was applied.

Past and Recent Occupational Mobility

Of the eight explanatory variables introduced in the model for occupational mobility during the previous two years (see table 9-3), five turned out to be significant: region (R), public/private establishment (PPE), level of skill (LS), age (A), and monthly salary (MS). The coefficient for region was expectedly negative. Since many establishments (public or private) in the Northern and Southern regions had been recently established or expanded, a significant portion of the Saudi workers in these regions were new to their current occupation. A relatively high proportion of them were also newcomers to the two regions. The negative coefficient of the PPE seems to reflect the recent increase in public recruiting of Saudi labor relative to that in the private sector. The coefficient of level of skill is positive and highly significant. Workers with higher skill levels seem to have greater opportunity and flexibility for changing their occupations.

Age was found to be negatively related to occupational mobility because of the relative cost of changing one's occupation. Aside from the social and psychological cost of investing in retraining at an older age, the payoff seems to be limited by the years remaining until retirement. This is a rational decision within a life-cycle framework. Finally, monthly salary (MS) was found to be significant and negatively related to occupational mobility. Such a finding is expected since changing occupation implies a loss of some seniority relative to peers in the new occupation. The coefficients of education, home ownership, and income adequacy were not significant.

Table 9-3. *Change in Occupation during the Previous Two Years: Saudi Establishment and Household Workers, 1978; Multivariate Analysis*
(probit estimates)

Variable	Establishment sample		Household sample	
	Full model	Reduced model	Full model	Reduced model
Intercept	1.190	0.802	0.545	−0.458
	(2.390)	(2.453)	(0.636)	(−1.035)
Region	−0.590	−0.610	−0.138	−0.053
	(−2.480)	(−2.564)	(−0.573)	(−0.227)
Public/private				
establishment	−0.530	0.552	—	—
	(−2.650)	(−2.750)	—	—
Level of skill	0.780	0.784	0.255	0.287
	(4.600)	(4.642)	(0.926)	(1.067)
Age	−0.160	−0.156	−0.098	−0.109
	(−4.500)	(−4.642)	(−0.926)	(−1.067)
Education	0.080	0.079	0.074	0.076
	(1.250)	(1.235)	(0.625)	(0.666)
Monthly salary	−0.130	−1.140	−1.123	−0.090
	(−2.220)	(−2.030)	(−1.388)	(−1.087)
Home ownership	0.050	—	−0.330	—
	(0.390)	—	(−1.465)	—
Income adequacy	−0.100	—	−0.186	—
	(−1.150)	—	(−1.129)	—
Number of observations	583	583	269	269
Mean dependent variable	0.185	0.185	0.119	0.119
Degrees of freedom	8	6	7	5
χ^2	76.4	74.7	12.9	10.0

— Not applicable.

The short form of the model used the five significant explanatory variables and education (see the second column of table 9-3). No significant changes occurred in any of the coefficients or in their level of significance. Again, the findings seem to be robust, at least for this sample.

The same models and procedures used in the analysis of the establishment sample were applied to the household sample (see the last two columns of table 9-3). Significant differences between the findings of the two samples exist. In the full model, although the coefficients have the expected signs, none were significant. In the reduced model, age was the only significant variable. This low predictive power of the model for the household sample is reflected in the low χ^2, which was 12.9 as compared with 76.4 for the establishment sample full model.

To examine occupational mobility during the previous four years (that is, with larger average mobility), the same model and procedures were applied. The findings reported in table 9-4 do not differ much from those of recent mobility reported in table 9-3. The only substantive difference was that the region variable became insignificant although it retained the same negative sign. This was expected on a priori grounds because

Table 9-4. *Change in Occupation during the Previous Four Years: Saudi Establishment and Household Workers, 1978; Multivariate Analysis*
(probit estimates)

Variable	Establishment sample		Household sample	
	Full model	Reduced model	Full model	Reduced model
Intercept	1.040	0.632	−0.068	0.181
	(2.290)	(2.112)	(−0.089)	(0.447)
Region	−0.290	−0.315	−0.004	−0.009
	(−1.30)	(−1.438)	(−0.017)	(−0.042)
Public/private establishment	−0.440	−0.452	—	—
	(−2.520)	(−2.627)	—	—
Level of skill	0.740	0.745	0.401	0.369
	(5.050)	(5.121)	(1.669)	(1.555)
Age	−0.088	−0.083	−0.143	−0.145
	(−2.930)	(−2.831)	(−2.860)	(−2.991)
Education	0.130	0.130	−0.038	−0.021
	(2.230)	(2.207)	(−0.350)	(−0.197)
Monthly salary	−0.160	−0.144	−0.079	−0.090
	(−3.010)	(−2.812)	(−1.014)	(−1.189)
Home ownership	0.110	—	−0.176	—
	(0.900)	—	(−0.862)	—
Income adequacy	−0.120	—	0.092	—
	(−1.420)	—	(0.636)	—
Number of observations	583	583	269	269
Mean dependent variable	0.266	0.266	0.178	0.178
Degrees of freedom	8	6	7	5
χ^2	72.6	69.3	16.7	15.3

— Not applicable.

regional development in the North and South is relatively recent. The effects of other variables were the same as in the models for occupational mobility during the previous two years. The case of the household sample was also similar (third and fourth columns, table 9-4). The only significant variable was that of age.

Change in Industry during Previous Two Years

Another indicator of mobility is the worker's move from one industry to another. Because of the changing structure of output and its sectoral composition, it is important to find out whether workers move across sectors when they change jobs. What are the main factors behind such a decision? The same model applied in the analysis of past occupational mobility was applied to industry change (see table 9-5). The findings for the full model and the short model for both the establishment and the household samples are quite similar to the findings of past occupational mobility. It seems that the same rationale applies in occupational as well as industry change. Both are facets of changing jobs. Accordingly, the findings imply that the changing of occupation or of industry is incidental to the process of job change.

Conclusions

The results presented in this chapter show strong evidence of occupational mobility among Saudis both in the past and at the time of the survey. The results also show evidence of accelerated mobility, from both the establishment worker sample and the household sample. Thus, while during 1974–75 about 9 percent of the establishment sample and 6 percent of the household sample changed jobs, during 1976–77 the numbers increased to 19 and 12 percent, respectively. In 1978 the figures for those with plans to change were 20 and 10 percent, respectively. The implications for the labor market in Saudi Arabia are clear: members of the Saudi labor force are not reluctant to change their jobs. A sizable segment is willing to change in the future. Such conclusions, however, must be placed in their proper context. The four years preceding the sample survey, which was carried out in 1978, witnessed unusual developments following the sudden jump of oil prices in 1973. The subsequent demand for labor not only shifted upwards, but also accelerated, closely following the pace of economic activity in the kingdom. Thus, the acceleration of occupational mobility of Saudi labor has been closely associated with an acceleration of the demand for labor at large.

Table 9-5. *Change in Industry during the Previous Four Years: Saudi Establishment and Household Workers, 1978; Multivariate Analysis* (probit estimates)

Variable	Establishment sample		Household sample	
	Full model	Reduced model	Full model	Reduced model
Intercept	2.290	1.693	0.651	-0.529
	(4.87)	(5.522)	(0.726)	(-1.167)
Region	-0.920	-0.831	-0.120	-0.030
	(-4.040)	(-3.737)	(-0.477)	(-0.122)
Public/private establishment	-0.490	-0.500	—	—
	(-2.790)	(-2.876)	—	—
Level of skill	0.200	0.198	0.074	0.124
	(1.440)	(1.433)	(0.259)	(0.451)
Age	-0.200	-0.211	-0.086	-0.100
	(-6.560)	(-6.960)	(-1.540)	(-1.816)
Education	0.150	0.145	0.167	0.162
	(2.550)	(2.410)	(1.370)	(1.374)
Monthly salary	-0.170	-0.149	-0.187	-0.143
	(-3.210)	(-2.895)	(-1.985)	(-1.630)
Home ownership	-0.280	—	-0.383	—
	(-2.180)	—	(-1.605)	—
Income adequacy	-0.100	—	-0.222	—
	(-1.280)	—	(-1.264)	—
Number of observations	543	543	241	241
Mean dependent variable	0.365	0.365	0.124	0.124
Degrees of freedom	8	6	7	5
χ^2	119.0	113.2	14.3	10.5

— Not applicable.

In the process of occupational mobility, particularly in the establishment sample during 1974–78, educational and skill levels have acted as stimulants, while age, salary, and the type of establishment acted as deterrents. A focus on the more recent years (1976–78) shows skill level to be the only stimulant and region, age, salary, and establishment type to be the deterrents. Thus, as occupational mobility accelerated, education lost its significance as a stimulant, while regional location gained significance as a deterrent (undoubtedly because of increased development activities in the North and South).

With regard to occupational mobility in the future, about the only variable shared in common with past mobility is that of education. Educated individuals tended to be more occupationally mobile and might be expected to continue to be so in the future. It is instructive to note, however, that a whole range of noneconomic variables assumes special significance in explaining future mobility: home ownership, job satisfaction, perception of income adequacy, and modernity (a proxy for which is the number of durables owned). In view of the nonsignificance of such economic variables as skill level, age, training, or monthly salary, the results are quite revealing. The implication is that in a tight labor market, Saudis have a significant propensity to move among occupations mainly because of noneconomic factors.

Notes

1. For a discussion of these ideas, see David A. Turnham, assisted by Ingelies Jaiger, *The Employment Problem in Less Developed Countries*, Employment Series no. 1 (Paris: Development Centre, Organisation for Economic Co-operation and Development [OECD], 1971). For various views on the subject and an indication of the historical development of the field, the following constitute a representative selection: P. M. Blau, J. W. Gustad, R. Jesser, H. S. Parnes, and R. C. Wilcock, "Occupational Choice: A Conceptual Framework," *Industrial and Labor Relations Review*, vol. 9 (July 1956), pp. 531–43; Jagdish Bhagwati and T. N. Srinivasan, "On Reanalyzing the Harris-Todar Model: Policy Rankings in the Case of Sector-Specific Sticky Wages," *American Economic Review*, vol. 64 (1974), pp. 502–08; Karl-Olf Faxen, *Monetary and Fiscal Policy under Uncertainty* (Stockholm: Almqvist and Wiksell, 1957), pp. 181–207; G. S. Fields, "Rural-Urban Migration, Urban Unemployment and Underdevelopment, and Job-Search Activity in LDCs," *Journal of Development Economics*, vol. 2 (1975), pp. 165–87; E. M. Godfrey, "Labor-Surplus Models and Labor-Deficit Economies: The West African Case," *Economic Development and Cultural Change*, vol. 17 (1969), pp. 2–391; J. R. Harris and R. H. Sabot, "Urban Unemployment in LDCs: Towards a More General Search Model," chap. 2 in "Essays on Migration and the Labor Market in Developing Countries," R. H. Sabot, ed., Proceedings of a Conference (Washington, D.C.: World Bank, 1978; processed); J. K. Hart, "Informal Income Opportunities and the Structure of Urban Employment in Ghana," *Journal of Modern African Studies*, vol. 11 (1973), pp. 61–89; R. A. Lester, *Adjustments to Labor Shortages* (Princeton, N.J.: Princeton University Press, 1955); H. Makower, Jacob Marschak, and H. W. Robinson, "Studies in Mobility of Labor: A Tentative Statistical Measure," *Oxford Economic Papers*, no. 1 (October 1938), pp. 83–123; "Studies in Mobility of Labor: Analysis for Great Britain, Part I," *Oxford Economic Papers*, no. 2 (May 1939), pp. 70–97; and "Studies in Mobility of Labor: Analysis for Great Britain, Part II," *Oxford Economic Papers*, no. 4 (September 1940), pp. 39–62; L. G. Reynolds, *The Structure of Labor Markets* (New York: Harper 1951); R. E. Sawyer, "Labor Migration, Relative Wage Levels and Unemployment in Less Developed Countries," *American Economist*, vol. 18 (1974), pp. 55–62; William F. Steel, *The Intermediate Sector, Unemployment, and the Employment-Output Conflict: A Multi-Sector Model*, World Bank Staff Working Paper no. 301 (Washington, D.C.: World Bank, 1978); J. E. Stiglitz, "Alternative Theories of Wage Determination and Unemployment in LDC's: The Labor Turnover Model," *Quarterly Journal of Economics*, vol. 88 (1974), pp. 194–227; E. W. Thorbecke and E. J. Stoutjesdijk, *Employment and Output* (Paris: OECD, 1971); and M. P. Todaro, "A Model of Labor Migration and Rising Unemployment," *Journal of Development Economics*, vol. 3 (1976), pp. 211–25.

10. Review and Outlook

THE PRINCIPAL OBJECTIVE of this study was to provide some empirical data to identify and explain the behavior of the labor market in Saudi Arabia, particularly in a regional context. This involved measurement of the existing regional distribution of labor and assessment of labor mobility among and within the kingdom's five regions. As the pace of growth and development varies among regions, the associated labor market adjustments also vary. An understanding of these labor market adjustments is crucial for manpower planning that would appropriately integrate regional and national development plans.

Many policies for human resource development contained in the second development plan were based on some explicit or implicit assumptions about the response mechanism of the labor supply and the structure of the labor market—for example, the social, economic, and information constraints on labor mobility and adaptation. Such assumptions, important as they were to the efficacy of the various policy options, were nevertheless without adequate empirical foundation.

An important objective of this study, accordingly, was to examine national and regional institutional rigidities in the labor market that may reduce its potential development or hinder its adaptive capacity to deal with the pressure of increasing capital expenditures on the supply and demand of local and foreign labor. Specifically, the study attempted to ascertain the potential growth and adaptive capability of the labor market in three major areas: wage determination, geographic mobility, and occupational mobility. In addition, the study sought to generate information on some elements that would be susceptible to policy-induced change and to examine their influence on the functioning of the labor market. These elements are the system of information flows, public and private, relevant to job search and location; the pattern of incentives and rewards; and the process of skill formation for existing labor (formal and informal training) and for new entrants to the labor market (education).

Findings and Policy Recommendations

Some of the findings supported existing knowledge about the labor market in Saudi Arabia, some contradicted widely held views about that market, and some covered previously unknown territory.

Findings which supported existing knowledge pertain to the dynamic nature of the labor market, the strong possibilities for growth in nearly all the sectors of the economy, the significant role of government, the increase in employment benefits, and the labor constraint, especially the shortage of skills, on potential economic growth.

Contradicting widely held views were the findings on the extent of interregional labor mobility and on the role of tradition in shaping labor decisions. Contrary to previous expectations, migration of labor among regions was almost nonexistent, while significant movement existed within regions. And in spite of traditions, market considerations dominated many labor decisions, especially mobility and wage determination.

Data on hitherto unfamiliar grounds were also reported. One out of every three working Saudis was employed in the informal sector (self-employed or working for a relative). Over 90 percent of Saudi workers had no formal contracts. Occupational mobility among Saudis was not only significant, but also accelerating in recent years, mainly because of a strong demand for labor in general and for Saudi labor in particular. Most job search information was acquired in traditional ways (direct walk-in and word of mouth). Pre-job and on-the-job training, though important in wage determination, was available only for a small minority of the labor force, with apparent disparities among regions. Education and training turned out to be highly viable economic investments in the development of the Saudi labor market since their positive effects were seen clearly in the analysis of wage determination. In addition, they influenced the processes of job search, geographic mobility, and occupational mobility. Although school enrollments at various levels expanded significantly in recent years, further expansion was expected in the future, as Saudi parents showed a strong commitment to educating their children, both male and female. The implications of such developments for skill formation are self-evident. The majority of Saudis approved of female employment, but not without some qualification. Whether these factors combined (expansion in female education and approval of female employment) would result in substantial expansion of female employment in the future remains an open question.

Government-Labor Relations

Despite a strong commitment to a free economic system, the government exerts significant impact on the labor market, through direct and indirect means (chapters 1 and 5). The government enacts legislation regulating a wide range of labor affairs from maintenance to development to importation. It employs directly tens of thousands in civilian sectors, in addition to those in the military. It influences labor demand indirectly through its massive development expenditures. It affects labor supply directly through importation of expatriates and on-the-job training programs, and indirectly through its educational programs and expenditures, among other things. For these reasons, the study tried to identify labor-related areas which are particularly policy-sensitive and which might become the focus of future action programs. Whatever their content, it is clear that such action programs can be carried out effectively only through increased coordination between the government agencies involved in human resource development and allocation (such as the Ministries of Planning, Labor and Social Affairs, Education, and Interior and the Institute of Public Administration). Within the framework of the third development plan, subsequent to the 1978 study, the government has established a national coordinating agency for manpower issues.

Job Market Information

Unlike traditional societies, the labor market in Saudi Arabia is a dynamic market. Conditions of demand and supply changed dramatically in recent years. The demand for labor continues to change in quantity and quality because economic activities keep expanding briskly (chapter 4), and the supply of labor continues to respond to such changes. Saudis have entered the market in increasing numbers and with higher levels of skill (chapter 3). About half the Saudis who were working during 1978 joined the labor force for the first time since 1976. For those with previous employment, the market provided better jobs. And 25 percent of the job seekers had more than one alternative when deciding to accept new employment (chapter 5). Yet, as previous studies have shown, the new Saudi entrants were not enough to keep up with market expansion, hence the sharply rising demand for expatriates.[1] Against this backdrop of recent years, prospects for the growth of business and economic activities during 1978–80 were strong, especially for the large private establishments (chapter 9). While a third of those establishments expected to expand their sales by 10 to 50 percent during the two years 1979–80, another third expected to expand by more than 50 percent during the same period. As a result, job vacancies continued to persist, regardless of the required level of skill.

By comparison with a 1976 job vacancy analysis (the Critical Skills Survey), the share of the public sector in the high-level categories increased while the share of production workers decreased. In the private sector, two-thirds of the vacancies were in the production worker category. In addition, managers of public and private establishments (large and small) conceded that labor shortages constrained their growth. For these reasons, some attention was focused on the flow of information affecting the process of job search and location. The findings showed that despite the dynamism of the Saudi labor market, the information system was still highly traditional, based mostly on word of mouth or direct contact (walk-in). It was also found that 29 percent of total male labor was informally employed (self-employed or working for a relative), 59 percent formally employed, 5 percent retired, 5 percent studying, and 2 percent unemployed (chapter 5). Under such circumstances, a large number of the labor force may not have adequate access to full information about existing opportunities.

Accordingly, the most reasonable response would be the modernization of the local labor offices into labor exchanges, with improved and updated files, and a more efficient system of information. Given the high illiteracy rate and the lack of geographic mobility, there is a clear need to reach labor in remote areas or at the periphery of the modern sector by innovative means (such as radio, TV, and mobile labor-recruiting units) that rely less on the written word and more on the spoken word.

Working Conditions

Employment benefits, security, and labor conditions in general have improved significantly by comparison with the 1960s (chapter 5). For example, unemployment has almost disappeared, and fringe benefits have increased both in scope and variety to approach standards in developed societies. Improvements were still possible, however, in health insurance, disability benefits, retirement plans, and the provision of training opportunities. Another issue related to working conditions is that about 90 percent of the Saudi labor did not have, at the time of the survey (1978), a formal contractual arrangement with their employers. In the absence of trade unions in Saudi Arabia, the government has traditionally assumed the role of workers' spokesman and protector. The formalization of labor-employer relations should assist in the fulfillment of that role and in the resolution of possible conflicts.

For all these reasons, the government is continuously examining the system of employment benefits and labor conditions with a view to improving them and possibly enacting more comprehensive labor legislation at appropriate times. The first steps in this direction include the expansion and improvement of the staffing of the labor inspection function to better monitor the extent of employment benefits and their application as stipulated by law.

Changing Attitudes

While some evidence pointed to the dynamism of the labor market, other evidence pointed to the strength of tradition. Traditions affect the labor market not only by supporting a personalized process of job search, an oral system of information, and pools of informal employment, but also by shaping workers' preferences and attitudes (chapters 6, 7, 8, and 9). Saudi workers expressed distinct preferences for their residential locations, job security, public sector employment, strong family ties (as indicated by financial and social commitments), and a qualified approval for female employment. This traditional outlook, however, is matched by many other attitudes that indicate easy adaptation to the rapidly changing environment and the constant introduction of new work and life styles. It is very clear that the present generation of Saudis is in the throes of a phenomenal transition from tradition to modernity, albeit with distinct elements of cultural continuity, that matches the country's awesome achievements in economic development.

Some measures to help Saudis make the adjustment have been discussed above. Others may be directed to new fields, such as family and health care for children and women, in which extensive use can be made of educated women who are graduating in increasing numbers (chapter 3). This could mean the possibility of expanding female employment into specially designed regional or local family and health care programs. Specially relevant in carrying out such programs is the revealed widespread interest in female education, as distinct from support for active participation of females in the labor force (chapter 6).

Wage Determination

Although other studies have highlighted education's significant impact on the economy of Saudi Arabia as the country attempts to raise labor productivity, limit the foreign labor ratio, and reduce the extent of possible structural unemployment, this study found education and training to be central factors in determining wage rates and family incomes (chapter 7). Thus, for Saudis in the labor market, investment in skill formation through education and training is economically justified. Age in traditional societies usually indicates experience and is thus the main factor in wage determination. In Saudi Arabia, by contrast, although large-scale modernization is only a recent phenomenon, the effects of education and skill formation turned out to be more important than age. Wage differentials by occupation initially reflected age and educational differences. After adjustments for these factors, however, wage differentials by occupation continued to exist. Job responsibilities and characteristics were sought to explain the adjusted wage differentials, but they provided only a partial explanation. The pressures of demand on certain occupations, such as operative labor, provided another partial explanation. By comparison with the other explanatory factors, the regional variable, although statistically significant, was weak. Interregionally, there were no inherent wage differentials.

After an analysis of the education-occupation-age mix of workers, money wage rates were found to be higher in private than in public enterprises. Such differentials in money wages were somewhat counterbalanced by nonmonetary considerations in the public sector, such as security and prestige. Nevertheless, there is the inherent danger of a brain drain from government to the private sector if the present wage differentials continue into the future. Given the pivotal role of government in the country's development at present and in the future, it is recommended that the government explore alternative methods or programs to enhance its ability to compete in the labor market, especially for qualified workers.

Geographic Mobility

Geographic mobility was found to be not especially significant, particularly between regions (chapter 8). About 16 percent of the Saudi establishment workers, for example, moved to their 1978 residence during the twelve months prior to the survey, and another 12 percent between one and three years prior to that. When examined by destination, the vast majority of the reported movement (80 percent) was within the same region. Thus, about 3 percent of the total Saudi labor force moved between regions from August 1977 to July 1978. Age and home ownership were the significant variables in explaining recent and past mobility. With regard to plans to move, home ownership appeared significant but age did not. Other factors such as education, ranking of job location, skill formation, and satisfaction with residence figured prominently. Some variables such as education, skill formation, and home ownership are directly policy-sensitive. Accordingly, it follows that in areas where labor inflows are needed the government should further expand its education and training activities and perhaps extend housing facilities to Saudi labor.

Occupational Mobility

There was strong evidence of occupational mobility among Saudis both in the past and at present (chapter 9). There was also evidence of accelerated mobility: during 1974–75 those who changed jobs constituted about 9 percent of the establishment sample and 6 percent of the household sample, whereas during 1976–77 they were 19 percent and 12 percent, respectively. In 1978 the figures for those who planned to change jobs were 20 percent and 10 percent, respectively. The clear implication is that Saudis are not reluctant to change jobs. In the past, however, the acceleration of occupational mobility was closely associated with rapidly rising demand for labor at large. Whether demand for labor will continue to expand as rapidly in the future is clearly a policy decision. To judge from the third plan document, the government appears to have opted for significantly slowing down the pace of expanding the total demand for labor, although the demand for appropriately qualified Saudi labor to replace expatriates will continue unabated in the foreseeable future.

Among the determinants of occupational mobility during 1974–78, education and skill level acted as stimulants, while age, salary, and the type of establishment acted as deterrents. A focus on the more recent years (1976–78) shows skill level to be the only significant stimulant and region, age, salary, and establishment type to be the deterrents. Thus, with the acceleration of occupational mobility, education became less significant as a stimulant, while the development activities in the North and South made regional location more significant as a deterrent.

Education was about the only variable which was common to both past and future occupational mobility. Thus, the more highly educated individuals tended to be occupationally more mobile and would continue to be so in the future. However, a whole range of noneconomic variables— home ownership, job satisfaction, perception of income adequacy, and modernity (as measured by the number of consumer durables owned)— assumed special significance in explaining future mobility, whereas economic variables such as monthly salary were not significant. The implication is that in a tight labor market Saudis have a propensity to move among occupations mainly because of noneconomic factors. How tight the labor market will be in the future is a policy decision shown in other studies to be closely related to the choice of a non-oil GDP growth target.[2] Higher growth targets imply a tighter labor market. In the third plan document, target growth for 1980–85 was significantly below the rates achieved during the second plan years (1975–80). The implication is that the labor market in the 1980s will be less tight than it was during the late 1970s.

From Tradition to Modernity

This study presents no more than a fleeting snapshot of a society in the midst of a phenomenal transformation, as indicated by the title, *Saudis in Transition*. We can clearly capture the sense of movement and its direction, but where it will lead and when can only be guessed. The Saudis of tomorrow will be definitely more mobile, more educated, and more responsive to labor market opportunities than today. Possibly they will also develop a more flexible attitude toward acquiring and accepting middle-level skills and jobs. In this movement they will be increasingly incorporated in the formal, modern economic activities of the country and will probably use more sophisticated, less traditional methods of job search. Yet this quest for self-improvement does not imply an abandonment of traditional values. Far from it, the Saudi journey from tradition to modernity is along a path of cultural continuity; the roots of the culture strike deep in the country's history, with its special relationship to Islam, and anchor a sense of identity amid the rapidly changing kaleidoscope of the Saudi environment. The labor market aspects described here are but one facet of this fascinating transformation.

Notes

1. Naiem A. Sherbiny, "Sectoral Employment Projections with Minimum Data: The Case of Saudi Arabia," in Naiem A. Sherbiny, ed., *Manpower Planning in the Oil Countries*, supplement 1 to *Research in Human Capital and Development: A Research Annual*, (Greenwich, Conn.: JAI Press, 1981), pp. 173–206.
2. Ibid.

Index

Age: demographic analysis and, 34–35; family income and, 126, 131, 133, 135; literacy and, 41–42; mobility model and, 147, 154; occupational mobility and, 166, 167, 182; wage rates and, 115, 116–17, 120–23, 125, 126, 128, 130, 180; worker, 79–80

Agriculture, 36; labor demand and, 67; technical education and, 47

Census, 29, 31, 35

Central Department of Statistics (CDS), 8

Chenery, H. B., 25

Civil Service Board, 85, 87

Communications, 38

Competition, 16, 17, 19

Compound Manpower Planning Model, 6, 7

Construction: infrastructure, 157; labor demand and, 67

Coopers and Lybrand Associates, Ltd., 9, 11

Critical Skills Survey of 1976, 6, 7, 179. *See also* Skill levels

Demand for labor, 4; aggregate, 63–67; analysis strategy and, 23, 25–26; expatriates and, 22, 66–67, 178; market institutions and, 95; neoclassical model and, 16; sectoral, 67–72; spatial distribution of 19; wage determination and, 20

Demographic factors: forecasting, 6–7; limits on information concerning, 28, 29–30; population size and growth and, 29, 30–34; study and, 28–29. *See also* Population

Development plans: capital availability and, 3–4; education and, 53; education and training system (ETS) and, 49–51;

human resources and, 57–60; regional aspects of, 39; resource restraints and, 15

Earnings. *See* Income; Income model; Wage determination; Wage rates

Economic Commisssion for West Asia (ECWA, United Nations), 30

Economic growth: demand factors and patterns of, 25; migration and, 139; modernization and development and, 3–4; sectoral labor demand and, 67

Education: allowance for, 89; children and, 106–09; enrollments imbalance and, 52; human resource development and, 57–60; income and, 131, 133, 135; mobility and, 148, 166, 170, 177, 182; planning and management and, 53; qualitative improvements and, 53–54; school system satisfaction and, 82; skill formation and, 41–49, 97–98, 177; vocational, 49, 54; wage rates and, 115–17, 120–21, 125, 126–27, 129, 177, 180; workers and, 75–76. *See also* Training

Education and training system (ETS), 6; development plans and, 49–51; enrollments imbalance and, 52; expansion and, 52; future challenges and, 55; planning and management and, 53; qualitative improvement and, 53–54; training and, 54–55. *See also* Education; Training

Employers: government as, 85–89, 94; government role in labor and, 85–86; neoclassical theory and, 16; private sector, 11, 87, 88–89

Employment: aggregate labor demand and, 63–67; demand and, 25; expansion of Saudi, 34; participation rates and, 28–29, 31, 74; population figures and, 29; preferences and perceptions of workers and,

185

tion of, 93–94; socioeconomic perceptions of, 81; theory and, 16–18. *See also* Expatriate workers; Occupational (job) mobility; Saudi workers

Working conditions, 86, 179–80
World Bank, 6–7, 11, 39

Yemen, 33

The full range of World Bank publications, both free and for sale, is described in the *Catalog of World Bank Publications*; the continuing research program is outlined in *World Bank Research Program: Abstracts of Current Studies*. Both booklets are updated annually; the most recent edition of each is available without charge from the Publications Distribution Unit, Dept. B, World Bank, 1818 H Street, N.W., Washington, D.C. 20433, U.S.A.

Ismail A. Sirageldin is professor of population dynamics and political economy at Johns Hopkins University. Naiem A. Sherbiny is a senior economist in the Projects Department of the Europe, Middle East, and North Africa Regional Office at the World Bank. M. Ismail Serageldin is director, Country Programs Department II of the Western Africa Regional Office at the World Bank.